Exiting the Rat Race

ARE YOU RETIRING FROM, OR RETIRING TO?

Jeffry A. Vogel
with
Jon Vogel

CFG Trusted Advisors, Inc.
TOPEKA, KANSAS

Jeffry A. Vogel/CFG, Inc.
2820 Mission Woods Dr.
Suite 100
Topeka, KS 66614
www.cfgks.com

Book layout ©2013 BookDesignTemplates.com

Exiting the Rat Race/ Jeff Vogel. — 1st ed.
ISBN 978-1978012417

Contents

To my first two clients, my father and father-in-law.

By wisdom a house is built, by understanding it is established, by knowledge its rooms are filled with pleasant and precious riches.

— PROVERBS 24:3-4

Introduction

L ife has a way of coming at you from all directions. Isn't that true? If you are like me, we have this way of allowing other people and things into our lives that take us down paths that, quite frankly, we wished we would never have taken. Sometimes we reach a point where we begin looking for a way out. This may be happening to you right now, being at a crossroads of decisions to make, and wondering which path to take. This book is written for and directed to those who are preparing to retire or who have recently retired, but in a broader sense it applies to anyone at any time in life. This book is not a guide to the latest and greatest trends in financial strategies—too often I find the "fad" strategies are just dragging retirees further into a maze until, before we know it, the rat race is on, we're halfway down a path that goes nowhere and, with no way out, we're trapped. Instead, I have chosen to focus on the principles behind our decision-making in retirement.

The cover of my book shows a maze. If you were to look closely, you would see there is no way, once in the maze, to actually attain the prize. The system is rigged, let's say. What most people miss is the maze is not mandatory. It's not a requirement to be stressed, to feel lost, or to feel like you are getting nowhere. Instead, I want to encourage you to engage in what we have called at various times "thinking outside the box" or a "paradigm shift." It is too much for one book to lead you through every single question specific to your situation, so I am not even going to try. I do want to address some key areas in a retiree's life, how to approach them, and help you start thinking of what path might give you a clear direction and confidence in retirement, and hopefully help you find you are capable of living the dream you hoped for.

Question: "Are you retiring from or are you retiring to?" An old saying is, "Are you jumping from the frying pan into the fire?" I hope not. There are two ways to consider the first question. Here is what I have found in my conversations with retirees and those preparing for retirement. There are some who retire with the motive, "I am ready to begin a new chapter in my life," and have a well-thought direction they are going. Those who have planned it well succeed but those without a plan either fall into a new rat race or struggle with boredom. Neither is good. Their own identity takes a hit. There is another group who just wants out of the workplace environment. They can't take it anymore, and they jump, hoping they'll find their way.

I see any number of people from each of these situations in my office every day, and I've been working to help my clients on their own paths since I started my career in financial services in 1986 at the age of 29. I had decided that accounting, the field I got my degree in, was not for me. My first two clients were my parents and my wife, Sheryl's, parents—my father and father-in-law both retired that year. It was an admirable gesture to want to help their kids get started in a new career, but to entrust their retirements to me was truly noble. I dedicated this book to my father, Harold Vogel and my father-in-law, Robert Morlan, because they gave me the confidence to get started in the profession. They both have passed on after enjoying and living meaningful retirements, and I am truly grateful for them both personally and professionally.

My experiences helping them retire, though, also affirmed me in my path to be a fiduciary financial advisor, meaning a financial advisor who is legally obligated to act in the best interest of my clients as opposed to recommending products and strategies that primarily benefit me. I saw how helpful it was for my father and father-in-law to have an industry insider on their side.

Another gentleman for whom I am grateful is Vaughn Kimball. Vaughn was my mentor early in my career, and helped me find the way around my own personal "rat race." Not long after I started in my career, I asked him, "By the way, Vaughn, how old are you?" He said he was 83. I knew he was up in years, but had to know why he was still working. As a young man new to the profession, I asked "You aren't working because you *have* to, are you?" His answer has stuck with me all these years. He said, "NO, I don't *have* to work. Jeff, your clients will become your friends. I get to see my friends every day. I have lunch with them and golf with many of them. I travel when I want to." He was affirming me in my decision to choose this as a profession and a life. He gave me an example of loving your work and the people you serve. He finished with, "Why would I ever retire, when I already get to enjoy what everyone else does in retirement?" That same thought continues with me to this day. I have no personal desire to retire. My work is not a rat race— I am not a workaholic, and I maintain a good work-life balance, for I had a great example. Thank you, Vaughn.

Not everyone works in their dream job, however. Or, even for those who enjoy their work, perhaps there is a higher calling, a dream or unfulfilled passion. Then again, others have little choice when it comes to leaving their day job—companies restructure, personal health deteriorates, family outside of the office needs more physical attention... The purpose of my book is to provide a path to help my readers prepare for retirement or even repair the one they have already started. My desire is to get people thinking, to teach them not to give time to every so-called expert who has the next greatest strategy or product or hot stock tip. Maybe I should say it this way: one of my goals with this book is to help readers use common sense and make wise decisions.

Here are some questions to consider as you read this book:
- What do you value in life/what is of most importance?

- How are you going to generate the income to support your lifestyle?
- Will your income be in jeopardy at any time?
- What is your philosophy about investments and what is your current advisor's philosophy?
- What is your strategy to minimize current income taxes and future taxes at an unknown rate?
- How will you handle health care costs in retirement and protect your assets?
- What do you want your legacy to be? Everyone leaves one.

These are just a few questions to stoke the fire and help get your mind around this big topic. I have developed a process, "Your Re-tireWise Path," to help you think through and give direction to your answers. Each chapter addresses questions like those listed. Please enjoy this book, and may it help you exit the rat race.

Jeff Vogel
November 2017

CHAPTER ONE

Values and Dreams

It's 2009. A plain, 47-year-old unemployed woman with a plain name, Susan, appears on a popular show—"Britain's Got Talent." She steps out on stage, looking every inch like someone's kind but rather dowdy aunt. Simon Cowell, famous for his scathing criticisms, asks, "What's the dream?"

She responds, "I'm trying to be a professional singer."

The judges smile kindly. The camera pans the audience; a few audience members roll their eyes. Others smile tolerantly. Cowell asks, "And why hasn't it worked out before, Susan?"

"I've never been given the chance before, but here's hoping it'll change," she says brightly. The audience chuckles.

As the exchange continues, the audience gets more and more skeptical. More eyerolls, pitying smiles. When Susan says she'd like to sing like Elaine Page, the audience laughs outright.

If you remember this particular moment, you know what comes next. Susan Boyle lifts the microphone, pours out her heart, and speaks directly to anyone in the world who has ever had a dream.

"I dreamed a dream in times gone by
When hope was high and life worth living

I dreamed, that love would never die
I dreamed that God would be forgiving

Then I was young and unafraid
And dreams were made and used and wasted
There was no ransom to be paid
No song unsung, no wine untasted"

By the time "Susan Boyle, 47, unemployed" finishes "I Dreamed a Dream" from "Les Miserables," the crowd is on its feet, even the judges are actively cheering for her, and Simon Cowell's eyes look suspiciously wet.

In fact, even now, I play the clip from Susan's opening performance at my retirement seminars, and though my staff members have seen it over and over, we all still have an emotional response.

We all, in some way or another, can identify with the stricken Fantine's song from Les Miserables, and, perhaps even more, with Susan Boyle. We all are still dreamers at heart, or we ought to be. Most of us have been dreaming of retirement. Maybe you're dreaming of traveling. Maybe it's your dream to spend endless days on a lake, fishing or boating to your heart's content. Maybe your dream is elaborate; maybe you're looking forward to the day you can quit the 9-to-5 and instead start up a hobby store or a second-act business of some kind. Or maybe your dream for retirement is simple; maybe you are dreaming of the day that you can read every word of the newspaper and reach the bottom of your morning coffee mug at your own leisure.

What do all these dreams have to do with your investments? What does your love of model airplanes have to do with your 401(k), or spousal options on your pension? I'll tell you: Everything.

Here's why.

Think of the tools we use for retirement. This is what we often think of a lot when we think of retirement planning. You probably would say, 401(k)s, IRAs, stocks, mutual funds, real estate, annuities, bonds, life insurance, exchange-traded funds, etc. Those are our TOOLS.

Why do we have these tools? Products like municipal bonds or 401(k)s offer us certain tax advantages. Life insurance products offer us guarantees, such as annuities, which offer guaranteed income. Stock-based products give us growth opportunities, and bank products like our checking accounts give us liquid access to our funds. Those are the RESULTS we expect from our TOOLS.

But why do we want those results? There's the rub. Our RESULTS can help us fund other things in our LIFE. When I ask people in my seminars what matters most in life, the answers are quick to follow: family, grandchildren, freedom, health, income, volunteering, having a home, faith, purpose, hobbies. These, really, are our dreams. Our LIFE.

We put money into TOOLS to get RESULTS to fund our LIFE decisions. Our values really show up in our life priorities. Once we have our values straight, we get clarity on what tools to use.

So, what is the most important thing, the financial results, your tools, or the life you are able to build? I've never had someone tell me their TOOLS are more important than their LIFE priorities.

Instead of starting with the tools we have and looking at where we want to go, sometimes it's better to reverse-engineer our retirement process. It's kind of like with those wooden peg puzzles that became so popular a few years ago. It seemed like everybody and their grandkid got one for Christmas—they are like wooden versions of Rubix cubes. I saw the people who paid attention when they took them apart were more likely to figure out how to put them back together. That's what we're doing here, too—beginning with the end in mind. Think more about your dreams and your goals and your values, and what results you'll need in your finances

to make those dreams and values happen. Once you know what results you need, you can drill down into the specifics of what tools
might get you those results.

That's why it really does start with your dreams. As I like to say,
if you're not dreaming, you're dying. In fact, statistics back me up;
the forward-thinkers and dreamers, those who look to the future,
are more likely to live longer. Is that a surprise, once you really
think about it? I would say no. Life has a lot to do with our dreams
and values. If you look to the future, you have something to get up
for in the morning. In fact, one eight-year study showed those with
a great sense of purpose and fulfillment were less likely to die than
their unfulfilled peers.[1] In a way, that brings us back around to the
subject of the book. Are you retiring FROM something, or retiring
TO something? I think it's fair to say we all want lives that are
driven by purpose and meaning. And we find that meaning in our
dreams and in our values.

Values are the foundation on which we build our dreams, and
they dictate many of our actions. Have you ever acted in a way that
didn't reflect your deeper values? You feel pulled. You feel frus-
trated. It's just not a great way to live your best life, wouldn't you
say? So it is with retirement. We want our lives in retirement to
reflect our values. I find when our values are clear our decisions are
easy.

In my office, when I start with a new client to help them get
going on their retirement preparations, a lot of the time they sit
down and want me to give them a simple "yes or no" on retirement.
They want to talk money and returns, but how can I know what
they need based off a spreadsheet or a list of products? It may take a
while, but I have to get them talking, ask good questions and be an
astute listener, to tease out their dreams, goals and, ultimately, their

---

[1] Alexandra Sifferlin. Time. Nov. 7, 2014. "Having a Sense of Purpose Helps You Live
Longer." http://time.com/3568105/sense-of-purpose-live-longer/.

values. In my 30-plus years of doing this, I've had to get more and more creative with how to draw this information out. I noticed early on that sharing about myself and my own values sometimes helped draw the same information out of the person I am visiting with. Even now, I usually feature a photo of my family in the retirement seminars and presentations I give. It's a photo we took a while ago during one of our vacations in Mexico. It's a pretty good summary of some of my values—it's got my wife, children and grandchildren, all together, hand in hand, starting a day of fun in the sun. I can point to that photo and ask the people in my financial seminars if they have similar photos, either real or imagined.

I've gotten much better from when I was a young man right out of college. Back then, I loved the financial services arena because it appealed to my mathematical side, while also letting me work with real live people. Yet, despite the numerous casual conversations I had with clients back then, it took me a while to understand, once you get people talking, they begin to share what is important to them. Over time, I realized those are the areas that best reveal people's values, and I boiled it down to a process. Following is my values test, the five Fs, which I use to get people thinking about where their priorities really are. Take a second to think about your own answers to these as we go through—sometimes people even surprise themselves with their answers.

FAMILY

What are your thoughts toward your family? Would you consider close friends part of your inner circle, your "Circle of Trust"? What would you like to see happen in your family relationships? How are you communicating with them? What would you like for them to know about you? Do you want to be involved in their futures?

FINANCES

What do you want to have happen in this area? Do you have debt issues? Are there cashflow issues? Does your income keep up with your desired lifestyle? What would you like your finances to look like? What system or process would you like in place to manage this area of your life?

Do you describe yourself as a saver, or as a spender?

Are there things you are unsatisfied with in your finances?

FAITH

What's important to you in your faith? How are you exercising your faith? What kind of time do you like to spend in this area of your life?

Is this an area you'd like to see as a bigger part of your life?

FITNESS

What has to happen for you to be able to live the way you want? How would you describe your health and fitness level?

What kind of activities do you want to do, and how can you be sure you will be physically able to handle those things?

FUN

All work and no play makes Jack a dull boy! What does "fun" mean to you?

Do you want to travel? Have any hobbies? Do you want to keep working?

Each of these five Fs helps us reveal a person's priorities, their values and dreams. Ultimately, everyone we meet with wants to feel FREE and FULFILLED, but freedom and fulfillment come to people in different ways. For some people, church mission trips are the most important thing to help them find purpose, while other people want to fund a lavish home so they can entertain friends.

Recently, I was at a conference with about 700 other people. We watched some videos of conversations with people who recently retired. One of the couples had taken up playing the ukulele. I kid you not, they wanted to do something fun and different in retirement. The next morning to start things off, there was a piano player, later joined by someone walking on stage playing a guitar and then others were joining them with other musical instruments. Then I heard what sounded like ukuleles. You guessed it, out walks the retired couple from the video the day before playing in front of a large crowd. It's always nice to watch that sort of thing because it's evidence these people—in this case the crazy ukulele players—are still dreaming. And, if you're not dreaming, you're dying.

When it comes to our dreams and our values, I would be mistaken if I didn't talk about spousal planning. In the 21 years since I first founded CFG, I think this is one of the ways I've seen a lot of retirement dreams get off track before people even get started. It's important your dreams are up-to-date and coordinated with your spouse. Dreams are not a plan, but they are a first step in making a plan for a better life that's enjoyable. We all want dreams in retirement, not nightmares. So, maybe a couple has been talking about getting off the hamster wheel, but if they haven't talked about *why* and *what for,* it can make the *when* and *how* a moot point.

I have one friend who has been talking about retiring and jumping out of the rat race for years. He's got assets all over the place—different investments, different bank accounts, different insurance contracts. He hasn't sat down and made out much of a plan, though, because he and his wife can't seem to get on the same page about retirement. They have put off having a conversation about their values and their dreams. They could probably have retired by now, but this one conversation has both of them stalled out, still stuck in the maze.

When it comes to coordinating with your spouse, your goals, values and dreams should be:

- Mutually agreeable
- Well-defined
- Based in a joint purpose, or based in your values
- Up-to-date and recently discussed

On that last point, even if our values haven't changed, sometimes our goals and dreams do. I had a couple in my office with whom we discussed values. Their values were pretty well aligned. They seemed to have a lot of things together, and it was clear they had started planning for retirement early on and were ready to reap the rewards from decades of planning. Yet, not long into our conversation on goals and dreams, I asked, "What will your housing situation look like?" The husband said, "We're planning on moving to Florida." His wife's face said they were *not* moving to Florida. He took a look at her and confusion spread over his face. "We have a home in Florida. We bought that house years ago, aren't we planning to live there?" She responded, "Well sure, we *planned* to live in Florida, but that was 15 years ago! Now all my friends are here. I don't mind visiting Florida, but I am not sure I want to live in Florida!"

It may not always be Florida, but I cannot count the number of times I have heard that conversation play out. When your values are clear, your decisions are easy; married people need to have *joint* values. In one of my recent client visits, we were having this values conversation. Toward the end of the conversation, the prospective client made the suggestion that I should have a "Retirement Therapist" on staff. My reply was, "You know, that may be a good idea."

We all got a nice chuckle out of that. But it does ring true that retirement should have more consideration than just a yes or a no. When people are moving toward something, they enjoy more freedom than when they are focused on moving away from something. When we've aligned our values and dreams, our actions can be more reflective of those priorities, which can lead us to a better sense of accomplishment. Science even backs this up—it seems like every few years there is another research piece or another article that tells us the happiest people, even in retirement, are those who look forward to the future.

I mentioned I used to work for a large financial institution. I was successful; early on I got sucked up into management transfers. Each time a new position opened up above me, I got a boost up the corporate ladder and, since it was a national company, I got a nice moving stipend to truck my wife and three sons across the country to be in our nice, shiny new city. Every few years was the same story: a bigger office, a better position, a bigger team to manage, a new house.

My resume was impressive, but I felt the strain. My family didn't get to put down roots, and it was challenging my family values. I realized one of my sons had been through three different high schools. It was time to make a change. I called the powers that were and explained I was done. I was done climbing the corporate ladder, I was willing to trade my ambition for some semblance of permanency. I told them, as a Kansas native, that's where I wanted to be for the long term.

They offered a transfer to their Topeka office. I took it and, in a number of months, had quit the rat race in my own way by starting my firm, CFG, Inc. It's not that I wanted to quit working entirely, but I was tired of working in the fast lane, running around following someone else's game plan. In truth, when I reached a certain point on that corporate ladder and looked around, I saw my life wasn't in line with my values. So, in cutting the cord and branching out on my own, my values made my decision.

Isn't that, in a large part, how retirement is? I knew what I wanted to do when I left the big company. I wanted to really help people—on my own terms—to retire on *their* own terms. I wanted to work for and with people who shared my company's values of faith, family, freedom and, of course, fun. That holds true today. I look for my clients to have a real sense of purpose and happiness entering into retirement.

Because of the complexity and scale of retirement, and the implications of planning for it, it can make people feel insecure or unhappy, which is why people often put off making a plan. What helps take away these feelings of insecurity and unhappiness and the "unbalances" is to begin to simplify things. Starting with a goal, your dreams and your values, is empowering.

Plan to fund a retirement worth living, and follow a process to cope with the unexpected. Instead of thinking of the future as complicated, conflicted and confused, take some time to think of how you will use all of your intelligence, all of your energy and the skills you possess, because you've acquired a number of them. Your creativity. I have heard that people 55-plus are entering into their most creative years. I don't remember where I read that, but if this is a time where you could become more focused and channeled, then get ready!

I'll close this chapter on dreams and values by pointing us back to Susan Boyle. One of the mantras of our office is Clarity, Confidence and Capability. Susan Boyle had clarity about who she wanted to be—she wanted to sing like Elaine Page. She was obviously confident about pursuing her dream—she likely had many people who had supported her over the years—otherwise, how could she have had the courage to even get up on stage? And, as she proved once she clutched that microphone, she had an enormous amount of capability.

What we saw was a punchy few minutes of stellar singing and bravada, but behind the curtain of her performance was years of backstage work that she put in to improve to the point that she was good enough to make it. You don't get there without being clear on your values, and keeping dreaming.

CHAPTER TWO

Cashflow

N ow, before we get ahead of ourselves talking about the process of managing assets for retirement, we should take a second to address sort of a "preexisting condition" of retirement health: cashflow.

By cashflow, I mean the simple transaction in your household of dollars in, dollars out. The way you manage your cashflow can make or break your plans for retirement before you even get there. How?

Just like in business, cash is king, in personal economics, cashflow is king. Allow me to introduce an economic principle here, "The Law of Scarcity," meaning every financial decision we make is at the expense of another one. Money is a finite resource. Unless you are the U.S. Government and can print money (which has its own repercussions), our limited supply of money will affect the outcome of our financial decisions in retirement.

This is why it's so important to allocate our spending to the lifestyle we desire, both now and in the future. Do you want to drive the new, updated car now or would you rather keep your used, late model, nice-looking vehicle and be able to afford the trip you dreamed of and some good times in retirement? There is nothing wrong with the new car instead of the trip, but you need to take stock every once in a while and ask where your money is going and whether it matches your values. Are you living by default, as it comes to you? Or are you living with purpose?

So, do you know what your cashflow looks like? Do you have a system for managing it?

Before you roll your eyes or cast this book aside, you don't know what's coming next. You just think you know.

Many people have heard of the B word. Budget. In my office, couples come in and, whether they have a cashflow problem or not, they start grumbling about how they should do a "budget." For starters, I don't like or believe in budgets. How's that? There are spreadsheets, tracking every purchase, saving receipts... Too often, you spend more time tracking where your money went instead of directing where it needs to go, your intended desire or purpose.

I'm a fan of processes and systems, as I'm sure you already know. So, instead, I ask people to use a cashflow system to get a handle on their money. That's a "Save YourSelf Time, Energy and Money" SYSTEM. You don't have to have money problems to need a cashflow system. Some people need a system because their lifestyle outstrips their income sources—they're living in debt, and their money problems control them more than they control their money. But other people just want to know where their money is going. That's uncomfortable. By having a system in place, our good decisions are repeatable, all without asking ourselves every question about every dollar every time.

Now, to do this system, you're going to need a lot of fancy, technical software and sophisticated workbooks, right? Wrong! You just need a bank (or a credit union). See, most banks have the option of doing auto-payments. This is a total gamechanger, and you can put this to work for you. So, how would a bank-based cashflow system work? To do this, I am going to use my wife Sheryl and myself as an example since I developed it and she implemented it. Sheryl handles the money in our home (good idea, guys) so I thought it wise she tested it. We have never had a debt problem, but I always wanted to know where our money went.

Sheryl and I started budgeting in 1982 and hated every year of it. Finally, about 10 years ago, I developed a simple system for managing cashflow using what was available at most banks; auto-payments, automatic transfer between accounts and online bill pay.

Cashflow System

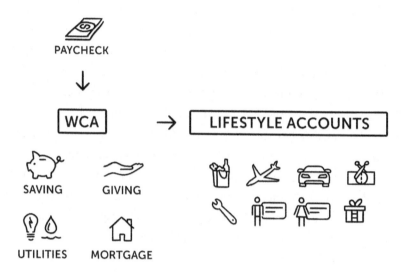

Step one was to have all income from take-home salary, investments and rents paid into a checking account we called the Wealth Coordinating Account (WCA). Out of this account, we had transfers occur automatically to the places that are top priority, before anything else. We are givers, so this meant first sending money to our church and other places we have a heart and passion for. Next was savings and investments, to support the idea of paying yourself first. Our mortgage was the next item that came out of our WCA. For clients who have other debt that needs to be paid off, I often suggest paying it automatically out of their WCAs. We then would transfer an amount to another checking account that we paid living expenses out of, the same amount every month.

Our living expense account was also set up automatically with online bill payments for utilities, cable and similar items. The real magic happens with other checking accounts that funds were automatically transferred to. These accounts were for groceries, home maintenance, auto maintenance, utilities (we did our own averaging), property taxes and insurance, gifts (a real problem when you have a lot of grandchildren!), vacations, and a Sheryl account and Jeff account (yes, we decided to each have "free money" to spend, no questions asked). There was an automatic transfer each month to these accounts and we lived by them. The account balances made our decisions for us. These accounts did not have checks attached to them because we did not want the ability to write checks on them. Our reasoning was that, if you had a checkbook for the account, you would need to balance them every month. We wanted to be low-maintenance. Some of them did have debit cards we used as cash, but no overdraft protection. That's right, the card was kicked out if you tried to overspend the account!

I called this system "The Smart Cash System" and it has worked wonderfully. Sheryl thought I was nuts in the beginning because, to her, it had looked complicated. But it really is not. With the technology today to check balances on accounts, it was very easy to know where you were with living expenses. It took a little time to set up at the bank, but to this day we still use this system. Sheryl will tell you, along with a number of clients who use it, without a doubt, it is one of the best tools I have given them. Many banks will do this without charging for the accounts. If your bank says they will charge you for using multiple accounts, find another bank.

This kind of a system holds you accountable, so you control your money and don't let your money control you. Particularly with the million financial phone apps today, you can check up on your money all the time. Instead of being like a budget and saying, "here's what I did," a cashflow system is about "here's what I can do"—no spreadsheet necessary.

The brilliance of having a system like this is in its simplicity. This is something you can totally do on your own—you don't need a financial advisor to help you. The reason I think it's important, though, is that I run into people with cashflow problems all the time in my business. How many New Year's resolutions are about finances and "getting control" of people's income versus outflow? The earlier you can manage your money, the better set up you will be. With a system like this, it's reactive. You can revisit your setup every few months (I usually suggest revisiting it every six months) to be sure you like the way things are going or make changes as life changes, but having a system (instead of a line-item dictatorship of a budget) can be a relief, particularly for couples.

It's always harder when a couple comes in and are used to considering His money vs. Her money instead of thinking of it as Our money. Often, it reflects they haven't gotten squared on that whole topic from Chapter 1—dreams and values. But, regardless, by agreeing to a system for allotting money equitably, couples can find a lot more financial harmony. As my son, Jon, who works with me in this practice, has said, "Having a smart cash system in place just takes so many money arguments out of the picture."

Once you've got a plan in place to deal with your cashflow, and once you know that you aren't self-sabotaging, then you're ready to dig into the real process of planning for retirement, a process we here at CFG like to call Your RetireWise Path.

CHAPTER THREE

RetireWise Investment Plan
by Jon Vogel

Jon Vogel is an Investment Adviser Representative of CFG Trusted Advisors, Inc. Jon re-joined his father in the office in 2013. At CFG, Jon takes a leading role in crafting the company's approach to investing.

I love mountains —I love mountaineering, mountain air, mountain rains and mountain views.... even pictures and paintings of mountain views. I don't live in the mountains—I live in Topeka, Kansas, where my wife, Brittney, and I have most of our family within an hour's drive. But the mountains are only an 8-hour drive away. Before I was married and had kids, I used to spend a lot of time in the Colorado Rockies. "God's country," I call it.

You may be wondering how my love of the mountains ties into the investing step of Your RetireWise Path. Well, in addition to my love of mountain-based recreation, my experiences there have also taught me some solid life—and investing—principles. I have learned, for instance, how to respect nature and act wisely—if you've ever had altitude sickness to any degree of severity, you may get an idea of what I'm talking about. I learned the lesson of better planning beforehand, and investing in better tools, after I went on an off-trail hike, a very long distance from food or water with only a hand-pump water filter. By the way, one of those pumps won't do you much good if after each hill and valley you go over there isn't any water... even if on your topo map you may think there should have been.

Perhaps my most formative mountaineering experience, and one that brutally taught me the necessity of planning for the unexpected, was when I was caught alone in an unexpected blizzard. I was on the peak of the Mount of the Holy Cross by Aspen—a 14er (a peak of at least 14,000 ft. in elevation), on what was supposed to be a long day-hike with fairly warm and clear weather. I was wearing shorts and a T-shirt, though I did have a very light rain jacket in my bag. I had about 30 ounces of water and next-to-no food. I reached the top just fine, but I realized once the blizzard hit that I didn't have the tools to get down. I tried to descend due to the extreme summit conditions, but if you've seen a boulder field atop a Rocky Mountain 14er, you'll know what slowed and stopped me. I had literally next to no visibility, nothing for shelter and horribly inadequate clothing. On my halting way down, I found a father and daughter team who had brought "just-in-case" supplies. They were going to do the safe thing and wait out the storm. I couldn't. I hadn't prepared for this—continuing down the mountain was a terrible option, but it was the only one I had. I thought afterward (yes, I'll ruin the surprise ending...I lived to tell the tale!), about my objective for that trip. I had been concerned only with reaching the top. My parents had told me before that their objective for me wasn't for me to reach the top, it was for me to safely return.

Because I lived, the experience made me wiser. But I would not have needed that sort of experience had I heeded the words of an old mountain man I met in my journeys who ran an outdoors store. He told me to always pack for the whole journey. He said, "Think through your journey, having thought through all of the stages. The way up, down, over streams, multi-day trips, and expected weather conditions all change the way a mountaineering pack should be packed. This way, if ever caught in a situation, you can quickly, easily and efficiently access what you need to without further endangering yourself...all because and only because you were able to plan well in advance."

What has really allowed me to pack well now versus 15 years ago is how many treks I've been on.

We're now departing the mountains and I'll set to the task of explaining how this fits into investments. The very idea of investments makes most people think of Wall Street, investment bankers, stocks, bonds, risk, possible reward, possible loss. For a small number of people, all of this sounds exciting and enticing. For most others, it is mixed with fear and doubt, yet also feelings of necessity as far as having money in the market. Sometimes people see the reason of staying in the marketplace because they feel they must at least keep up with or outpace inflation. They see it as a necessary evil. A lot of this fear is rooted in the complexity of "the market."

So, rather than worrying about how the complexities of micro vs. macroeconomics could affect your investments, it's more important to understand a few basic principles around investing, and then follow a process to mitigate the risks that each of those principles pose.

Average vs. Actual Returns

This brings us to the first of four topics I wanted to briefly touch on in this chapter, which is average returns versus actual returns. The concept is really quite simple, and yet it is not known by most investors, and even some professionals! Here is the first and simplest example: You have $100,000 and get a 10 percent return year one, and a 10 percent loss year two. What is your is your average return? Zero percent. What is your actual return? A 1 percent loss!

This is using small swings like 10 percent. When you throw in a negative return of 53 percent, which the S&P 500 Index reflected between Oct. 15, 2007, and March 2, 2009—which is just a year and a half—you get a lot bigger difference between average and actual returns. Just remember, the more volatile the returns, the bigger gap between average and actual returns.

Now let's use another example. Imagine that your company 401(k) has just two investment options. Portfolio 1 and Portfolio 2. Portfolio 1 has an average return of 6.16 percent from 2000 through 2016. Portfolio 2 has an average return of 6.05 percent during the same period. Which would you choose? Probably No. 1, right? Its return is higher. But let's find out a little more. Portfolio No. 1 is just the S&P 500 index, which has no expenses. Portfolio No. 2 has a higher expense and not a recognizable name, but it still produced what is essentially the same average return. Now which would you choose? Probably still the first one, right? Okay, enough talk, a picture is worth a thousand words...well, maybe the following is not a picture, but how about the following chart?

Returns or Volatility? Portfolio 1			
Year	Market Performance	Year	Market Performance
2000	-9.10%	2009	26.46%
2001	-11.89%	2010	15.06%
2002	-22.10%	2011	2.11%
2003	28.68%	2012	16.00%
2004	10.88%	2013	32.39%
2005	4.91%	2014	13.69%
2006	15.79%	2015	1.38%
2007	5.49%	2016	11.96%
2008	-37.00%	Average	6.16%

Notice that when it's up, it's really up. Just look at 2013, a 32.39 percent return! And when it's down, it's really down. Take a gander at 2008. Down 37 percent...yikes. Think this makes some people question pulling the plug? Becoming more conservative or going to cash for a good portion?

Now let's look at Portfolio 2.

Returns or Volatility? Portfolio 2			
Year	Market Performance	Year	Market Performance
2000	2.68%	2009	14.55%
2001	0.24%	2010	10.77%
2002	-3.14%	2011	2.00%
2003	15.78%	2012	13.84%
2004	7.68%	2013	17.44%
2005	3.66%	2014	7.03%
2006	8.37%	2015	-0.42%
2007	3.65%	2016	9.58%
2008	-10.63%	Average	6.06%

Portfolio 2 has drastically lower volatility. It's not the same roller coaster Portfolio 1 is. Knowing what you now know about volatility, and probably even just from seeing the smoother ride between the two portfolios without really giving up any average return, you very may well choose Portfolio 2.

I kind of look at the two like this: Would I rather go on a mountain hike on a peak or range known for its tranquility, views and nice weather, or go climb one in which the peak gets heavier storms and harsher conditions more often than most? For some, this decision comes down to a preference based on personality. Most investors, if they have the choice, go a less "stormy" route because of fear of loss, perhaps because of life circumstances, the need for liquidity, or because of their proximity to retirement.

Now let's dig a little deeper and show what happens when money is applied.

Returns or Volatility $1M Initial Investment—Portfolio 1		
Year	Market Performance	Account Balance
2000	-9.10%	$909,000
2001	-11.89%	$800,920
2002	-22.10%	$623,917
2003	28.68%	$802,856
2004	10.88%	$890,207
2005	4.91%	$933,916
2006	15.79%	$1,081,381
2007	5.49%	$1,140,749
2008	-37.00%	$718,672
2009	26.46%	$908,832
2010	15.06%	$1,045,702
2011	2.11%	$1,067,767
2012	16.00%	$1,238,610
2013	32.39%	$1,639,795
2014	13.69%	$1,864,283
2015	1.38%	$1,890,010
2016	11.96%	$2,116,055
Average	6.16%	

Not bad at all! Double your money, right? Started with $1,000,000 and finished with $2,116,055. So, what did Portfolio 2 return in actual dollars? Let's see.

Returns or Volatility $1M Initial Investment—Portfolio 2		
Year	Market Performance	Account Balance
2000	3.18%	$1,026,800
2001	0.74%	$1,029,264
2002	-2.64%	$996,945
2003	16.28%	$1,154,263
2004	8.18%	$1,242,911
2005	4.16%	$1,288,401
2006	8.87%	$1,396,241
2007	4.15%	$1,447,203
2008	-10.13%	$1,293,366
2009	15.05%	$1,481,550
2010	11.27%	$1,641,113
2011	2.50%	$1,673,936
2012	14.34%	$1,905,608
2013	17.94%	$2,237,946
2014	7.53%	$2,395,274
2015	0.08%	$2,385,214
2016	10.08%	$2,613,717
Average	6.06%	

Hmmm…does that say $2,613,717? Just checking ☺. That's an additional $497,662. Think that lower volatility has more to do with successful investing, apart from being a skittish retiree? Maybe some of the roller coaster enthusiasts who are reading this are now having their economic-self nudging them in the side. Before you get all excited and ready to throw chips at Portfolio 2, please know that this is a hypothetical situation—we can't show you an actual client's return, but Portfolio 2 shows a portfolio that is diversified in stock indexes, a bond index and an annuity. There are certainly portfolios out there constructed for lower volatility, some done well and some done…well…not so well. But this is to portray a methodology of investing, not to make a recommendation of a portfolio.

From here I do want to address another of the key topics of this chapter, and that is fees and expenses.

Fees and Expenses

To tie this in to my mountain theme that I've committed to, I'll just say this, I've often *not* saved money by spending less. What I mean by this is, I bought cheaper gear and the gear wore out. The gear I've spent more on was engineered and built differently. It was built to last. On the other side of the coin, I've also spent plenty on some things that were not quite a fit for me, like a fancy and highly rated pair of boots that ended up just not being quite wide enough for me. Now I have a few-hundred-dollar pair of book ends. Basically, some things are worth the expense, and others are just not.

One of my favorite lines I hear as a financial professional is when good-mannered folks come into my office for the first time and lean toward me with a kind but cautious look and say, "Now Jon, I have to tell you, I'm very averse to fees." I just smile and perhaps even chuckle a little bit. I understand where they are coming from as I see the horrific fees in some portfolios—many people are unaware of the fees they're paying, and they often aren't getting the level of value and support that fee supposedly pays for in the first place. In addition to this, I also know most investors don't understand the difference between fees and expenses with investments, what all the expenses are in their current investments, and what services a fee is really supposed to be providing. By the way, these fees mostly pay for the construction of and lifelong maintenance of a financial plan that is always being reviewed under the then-current environment and adjusted if necessary. They are also to pay for the time it takes for an advisor to have a trusted relationship where they can help a client stick to their plan even under difficult circumstances, such as when the market is dropping or the client is having difficult circumstances in their life that cause them to consider abandoning their well-thought-out plan for reasons that don't fiscally add up. In other words, they are to be looking out for a client's best interests even if the client is in a place where they cannot see what that is for themselves.

Now, advisory fees can be all over the board. I've seen annual fees as high as 3 percent, and heard of some as low as 0.3 percent (though this was really not an advisory fee, but just an annual membership fee to be a part of some web-based model...and believe me, you get what you paid for with it). Let's just use 1.5 percent, as it is roughly the average of what I see when people come in from other advisory firms and they are larger accounts of somewhere around a million dollars or more. This fee can be for a good many things, including technological tools, but mostly it is for services.

Then there are these things called expenses, which everyone wants to keep as low as possible while not losing return. The expenses depend on what kind of investments are being used. Mutual funds, for instance, which became so popular during the 80s, have a number of costs involved. Investors typically think only of the common expense ratio, which is the percentage of your fund that you will pay for management fees, administrative fees and operating costs. Then, there are also transaction costs, which cover things like brokerage commissions, spread cost and market impact cost. There are also tax costs, cash drag and soft-dollar costs. For the sake of time and your sanity, we will only discuss expense ratios and transactions costs. We'll preserve at least some peace and tranquility on the mountain, so to speak.

Expense ratios are all over the board. Following are three different sources all pointing out the true, or "hidden costs," of mutual funds.

- Beverly Goodman. Barron's. March 2, 2013. "The Hidden Cost of Doing Business."
http://www.barrons.com /articles/SB5000142405274
8704356104578326293404837234
- Ty A. Bernicke. Forbes. April 4, 2011. "The Real Cost of Owning a Mutual Fund."
https://www.forbes.com/2011/04/04/real-cost-mutual-fund-taxes-fees-retirement-bernicke.html
- Anna Prior. The Wall Street Journal. March 1, 2010. "The Hidden Costs of Mutual Funds."
https://www.wsj.com/articles/SB1000142405274870
3382904575059690954870722

Each of these studies points to one thing. There can be a lot of costs associated with investing. Forbes cites a Morningstar study showing the average equity fund to have an expense ratio of 0.9 percent. Barron's cites a study of nearly 1,800 funds that had an average expense ratio of 1.19 percent. In that same study—a point that is cited across the articles—is that the trading costs, or transaction costs (buying and selling of securities within a mutual fund) have an average of 1.44 percent. That's more than the expense ratio! Roger Edelen, a finance professor at the University of California, Davis, who headed the study says, "The expense ratio is itemized, but trading costs are just a bleeding of assets. Investors think they know their funds' expenses, but they're really only seeing half the picture." And if only half the picture were really the full extent of it—according to the Forbes article, when other costs such as cash drag and soft-dollar cost are taken into account, the real costs are higher yet, even as high as 3 and even over 4 percent!

Now of course this is only a brief analysis of mutual funds. And this is not to say mutual funds don't have a place in a plan. They certainly can. But there are also many other investment instruments such as individual stocks and bonds, exchange-traded funds

(ETFs), real estate investment trusts (REITs), options and more. Each will have its own cost structure. It's just that mutual funds become a very obvious illustration of how unwary investors can be nickel and dimed.

Taxes

The next topic we'll discuss is one of the only two things that are said to be certain in life...death and taxes. Unfortunately, we'll be covering taxes. I'll keep this brief, as we do have an entire chapter dedicated to the subject, but a laser focus may prove helpful before we move on. Because I hope by now you share my love of mountains, I'll tie the topic of taxes back into the idea of having reserves, and having a plan with contingencies built into it to afford for many of the possible things that could prove the plan a failure.

Tax law, as we know, is always changing. This makes tax planning somewhat complicated. One way we at CFG work to mitigate this is through tax diversification. Tax diversification is not putting everything into any one instrument. For instance, if you have a lot of tax-deferred investments, you may be in for an unexpected tax bill when you take that money out. Don't buy into the myth that you will be in a lower tax bracket when you retire. How can a person know that? If they would tell me where they found their crystal ball, I'd be much obliged. And if their crystal ball actually worked, I'd be even more grateful, as I'd like to know when the next big market downturn will occur.

There is no doubt a high return is attractive at first glance, and while we've already discussed volatility, or averages vs. actuals, taxes are another one of the looming pits that could ultimately be eating up a good portion of your return. One way to control taxes is by using individually held stocks rather than funds, where applicable. With a stock, if you hold onto it for longer than a year and then decide to sell it with a gain, you get preferential tax treatment—you'll pay capital gains tax rates instead of ordinary income tax rates, meaning you'll pay a lower tax rate. This can be even more meaningful if you are in the 15 percent federal bracket or lower, which means there would be no capital gains tax on the realized gain. Another possible tax benefit to directly owning stock is having stock that pays a qualified dividend. These dividends are taxed at capital gains tax rates. At least, under current tax law this is the case. And we all know laws can and do change. Crafting strategies that balance returns and taxes is both an art and a science that we enjoy.

Diversification

The last, and certainly not the least, subject for us to discuss is diversification. I could never fully express the importance of this practice. Diversifying yourself is a lifelong, never-ending process. Ultimately, the person who never diversifies themselves never looks outside of themselves. And the one who doesn't look outside of themselves never sees others. The one who never sees others is never sharpened by others, or allowed to sharpen others and accomplish great tasks that people can only achieve together. This is why we should to seek appropriate council. This is why my profession exists: to form partnerships with others in optimizing their lives and helping them to obtain and/or protect the freedom they have worked so hard for.

I don't think I need to explain why financial diversification is so important. Most realize that if you have everything you own aboard one ship and that ship is sunk, you've lost everything. This is why it's not wise to have everything you own wrapped up in one company or one fund, or even multiple funds from one fund company. No one does everything well.

People have different ideas of what diversification looks like. Most think they are diversified if they have stock in a variety of different companies. To some, it means having a good blend of stock and bond mutual funds. To others, it's adding real estate into the mix. And to some extent these bring us closer to being more diversified in a positive manner than the people I've seen who are simply spread all over the place with what they have. Although I'd typically call these situations more of a mess than an example of diversification! True diversification is process- and system-driven to integrate and coordinate everything in one's financial life together like a symphony. When I put it that way, people then realize, "Wait a minute...no...I have no system for coordinating or integrating everything connected to me financially." But this is what it takes. It takes having a game board, putting all of your chess pieces on the board and beginning to think strategically with a model in mind. Only then can a person begin to see how an appreciated piece of land alongside an IRA and an insurance policy can impart incredible financial blessing to more people than just yourself. These are the kind of things that can arise from proper diversification.

There are different classes of wealth and I think it prudent to take a moment and mention them. Broadly speaking, there are two main categories and then many subsets of those categories. The two categories are statement wealth and contractual wealth. An example of statement wealth would be an investment account with stocks and bonds in it. Whatever the account balance reads on the statement is the wealth it represents. Pretty simple. The other category, contractual wealth, has mostly to do with the world of insurance. A level-term life insurance policy is probably the simplest example of this type of wealth. As long as the person who is insured pays their premium in a timely manner, they are privy to the benefit of the contract as it reads. If they die, their beneficiary will receive the stated death benefit of the contract. Annuity contracts are another example of contractual wealth. They have set values of what they are worth in dollar terms, but they also have benefits within them that are far more difficult to quantify than a stock account, which is simply worth whatever the market says it is at a given time.

Biases enter in strongly when people look at how they should diversify themselves. Some are biased toward stocks, others toward bonds, and still others toward insurance contracts. Each of these has its own strengths and weaknesses, just as all things do, and when a plan consists of only one of them, it will never reach its full potential. Each is built to accomplish certain things and when used improperly they can cause damage to a plan. I like to use the illustration of a sports car enthusiast who needs to pull a tree stump out of the ground. That person may be biased in their personal liking to a sports car, but even with all the power the sports car may possess, the engine is not torqued properly for the removal of tree stumps, let alone the frame of the car. What is needed is a truck built for towing capacity rather than speed. That person should look past their personal bias and what they like best and focus rather on the goal of the project, then determine what the best tool would be for accomplishing the task. So many let their personal biases interfere with their ability to achieve maximum potential in their financial lives.

This entire section can actually be summarized in one phrase that is age-old wisdom: Don't put all your eggs in one basket. We all know this, yet often people don't give it enough thought. They may think halfway through it and have a stock portfolio versus having only a single stock. But many stop short of reaching their full potential through true and proper diversification.

Don't think I forgot about the mountains. Diversification comes down to not spending your whole life on one mountain or type of mountain. What I mean by this—there are so many different kinds of mountains in so many different breathtakingly beautiful settings around the world. There are mountains that are volcanoes. There are mountains that are underwater. There are underwater volcanos. There are tropical mountains, arid mountains, timber-laden mountains, mountains by the sea, snow-covered mountains. This does not even exhaust the list. I happen to be a lover of the snow-capped Colorado Rockies, but that doesn't mean they would be the best choice for bringing along my children to a summit experience in the winter months. That would be a trip more suited for a southern mountain. Personal finance is somewhat the same. You need to wisely diversify yourself. I mentioned this before, but just having things spread all over the place is not diversification. And having everything you own under one asset class may not be a bad plan depending on how it is put together, but there are more effective routes to take to get you where you want to go in a better manner.

If I never ventured further than my personal preference of mountains, I would be missing the experience of a whole world of beauty. So, keep your eyes open. Don't lose the sense of adventure and dreaming the world around us can so often snuff out. Use your God-given mind and talents to maximize what you have. Form strong and wise relationships, and take care of yourself to be well.

CHAPTER FOUR

RetireWise Income Plan

O n Your RetireWise Path, investment strategies are built, of course, to help us take advantage of market opportunities and keep pace with inflation, but they primarily serve as a way to support your income plans. When you were in your working years, you were socking away money, trying to build up your nest egg, but you likely gave little thought to how you would get that money back and start receiving it once you retired.

It used to be this wasn't as much of a concern. After all, America had what we like to call the "three-legged stool" of retirement income. Between Social Security, pensions and personal savings, most people could count on having a decent "paycheck" in retirement. But now, both private and public pensions are on a steady and fairly steep decline. And you'd have to be actively trying to tune out the hubbub in Washington when it comes to the underfunded Social Security Trust Fund. That means the three-legged stool is looking more like a one-legged stool.

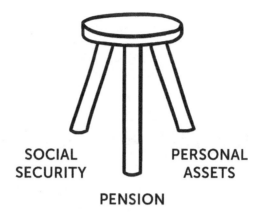

SOCIAL
SECURITY

PERSONAL
ASSETS

PENSION

The whole dilemma of a full retirement these days is you are no longer relying on an employer to send you a paycheck every month. Instead, you're responsible for creating your own monthly income based on those resources you accumulated over the years.

It's up to us to address the what-ifs of retirement. And I believe you need to what-if *everything.*

- What if the market underperforms for an extended period?
- What if you want to retire early and all your money is tied up in qualified plans?
- What if tax laws change?
- What if interest rates fluctuate (there are some who would like to see interest rates rise)?
- What if we have hyperinflation?
- What if you have limited access to your capital?
- What if the government changes its access rules for Social Security or tax-qualified plans?

I had a client, we'll call her Susan, who had been living for years as a widow. She and her husband had built up a sizeable nest egg, but she still lived in fear of losing her paycheck. Their previous advisor hadn't talked to them about how they would generate income from their assets when the time came to retire. It was this fear of the unknown and the chilling realization that everything was in one place that weighed heavily on Susan's mind. She worried, what if, in retirement, something happened to this one large asset in which they had stored up so much value?

This is the problem with just working toward your "retirement number." What I find from the people I work with in my office is that they are looking for a minimum number, a minimum amount in their retirement accounts on which they can survive. They ask, what is the lowest amount of assets I need to have saved in order to retire tomorrow and pay my bills? But is that really what you want in retirement? Think back to your dreams and your values. Is it your dream to pay your bills and no more? Is it your foundational value to barely scratch a living in retirement? No. Instead, most people's real desire going into retirement is to have no change of their current or intended lifestyle. They want to continue to build and protect wealth. They want to reduce the overall ailment of risk associated with traditional retirement planning approaches and reduce the overall risk associated with their investment portfolios. We want an increasing retirement income, a lower income-tax risk, more freedom from government regulations, diversified income sources, and to be in control.

Now, the reason our income and investments are separate topics in Your RetireWise Path is most of us don't want our income being contingent on market performance, right? If the market drops by 15 percent tomorrow, we don't want to have to reduce our lifestyle by 15 percent, do we?

An investment strategy is *part* of an income plan. Unfortunately, too many people focus on the wrong part.

Risks

Looking Out for the License-Plate Plans

Now, what I see most of the time is that people come in preparing for retirement and they will eventually draw Social Security, they *might* have a pension, and the rest of their money is tied up in tax-qualified plans, plans that sound a lot like a license plate.

- 401(k)
- 403(b)
- 457
- IRA

Traditional 401(k)s, 403(b)s, 457s and IRAs are tax-deferred, meaning you didn't pay taxes when you put the money into the account. That seems all well and good when you're starting out. You're saving up money! Your money is compounding! But Uncle Sam sure will get his cut. So, you will be taxed on that money when you pull it out, which means your deferral today is a tax liability tomorrow.

We're headed into 2018 and we have $20 trillion in government debt. One of the largest sources of funds in the U.S. are in qualified plans that have never been taxed. I don't want to belabor the point, but your danger meter should be approaching red. Keep your eye on those things; you may want to do some restructuring of your assets. No one knows what could or will happen. But it certainly is a large source for taxation that the rules can be changed on.

These accounts also aren't liquid before you turn 59 ½. That means, if you retire early, you don't really have total control over your money. That's certainly a problem when it comes to getting income.

There are a lot of traps and a lot of ways our money can be confiscated—but if we use these vehicles intelligently and along with other income sources, our other sources can help alleviate some of the disadvantages of qualified plans.

Unfortunately, today, much of the dialogue around income planning mostly revolves around the idea of what the "safe" withdrawal rate can be from a portfolio.

Withdrawal Rates

One of the misconceptions people have when they're looking at income strategies is about rate of withdrawal. They want to know, "If I have everything in the market, 50 percent equities and 50 percent bonds, how much can I take per year and still be safe?"

Media pundits and planners are telling you that the old "4 percent safe withdrawal rate" is now about 3 percent because of the bond environment. Yet, the person they often cite as coming up with the slightly-less-than-3-percent rate, Wade Pfau (professor of retirement income at the American College of Financial Services), says even a 3 percent rate of withdrawal gives you a 90 percent probability of success. That means you have a 90 percent chance of not running out of money in 30 years.[2]

Take a second to imagine you're taking a flight from Kansas City International Airport to Phoenix, Arizona. You board the flight, you stow your carry on and settle in your seat. The plane doors lock and the flight attendants do their safety presentation. The pilot comes on over the intercom, "Ladies and gentlemen, thank you for choosing our airline today. We've got a lovely ride ahead, clear skies, we shouldn't encounter any turbulence. We might even arrive early! Now, if you'll settle in, enjoy the in-flight entertainment, and relax as we make our way to the destination where we have a 90 percent chance of safely landing. Thanks again for flying with us today!"

---

[2] Walter Updegrave. Time Money. March 6, 2017. "Some People Have a Crazy Idea of What They Can Afford in Retirement." http://time.com/money/4689984/safe-withdrawal-rate-retirement/.

Would you want to be on that plane? I use this example in my seminars a lot because it takes a minute to tell the story, but it makes the point. I don't want a high probability that my income will "make it" in retirement. I want certainty.

When did the pundits stop thinking? Why is this the only way to look at income? Even if this is the way you have planned for income, it still doesn't address the problem of "what if the markets are down." Say you have a million dollars. In Year One, you take 3 percent. That's $30,000. Maybe the market made 3 percent that year, so you broke even. Yay! The next year, though, the market takes a 10 percent hit, leaving your portfolio at $900,000. Now, your 3 percent cut is $27,000.

Back to Wade Pfau, that guy who gets quoted in articles about safe withdrawal rates. He actually says to eschew this idea of only having an equity portfolio of stocks and bonds. Instead, in an editorial on Retirement Researcher where he was asked to compare insurance versus investments, he says:

"...retirement income planning is not an either/or proposition. We must step away from the notion that either investments or insurance alone will best serve retirees. Each tool has its own advantages and disadvantages. An entire literature on 'product allocation' has arisen, showing how a more efficient set of retirement outcomes can be obtained by combining investments with insurance."[3]

Taking Withdrawals from an Invested Account

Let's refer back to our two portfolios in Chapter Three. Remember, each portfolio had an average return of more than 6 percent.

[3] Wade Pfau. Retirement Researcher. April 12, 2016. "Which Is Better for Retirement Income: Insurance or Investments?" https://retirementresearcher.com/better-retirement-income-insurance-investments/.

Many advisors, radio talk show hosts and media pundits will use the historical average to arrive at a withdrawal rate that appears to produce a higher retirement income. I have had retirees come into my office who listened to this advice and are using high withdrawal rates. I have seen accounts such as the ones in Chapter Three, where the withdrawal rate was 5 percent. The thinking was, since the account averaged more than 6 percent, the owner should be able to withdraw 5 percent and still leave a cushion for growth. In the following charts, look at what happens to Portfolio 1 when we withdraw just 4 percent, or $40,000, out of the account each year.

Two things occur that create problems when making withdrawals from Portfolio 1, which are volatility in the portfolio and the sequence of returns. As you can see from the account balances, the retiree will have one heart-pounding ride taking withdrawals for income as they would see their account balance hit dangerous lows. Very few retirees would stay the course. Many would probably bail out of fear the accounts would run out of money.

I remember when my father and father-in-law both retired and gave me instructions for their accounts. This is what they both said, "Protect my principal, get me a decent rate of return and give me some income." Not a bad set of instructions.

Let's now look at Portfolio 2. Rather than relying solely on the ups and downs of the market, let's use a very diversified portfolio of some stocks, actively managed institutional funds, annuities and ETFs. Also, we'll use the same withdrawal rate of $40,000. As you can see, this type of portfolio can better handle market fluctuations.

Portfolio 1 Plus Withdrawals			
Year	Market Performance	Annual Withdrawal	Account Balance
2000	-9.10%	$40,000	$872,640
2001	-11.89%	$40,000	$733,639
2002	-22.10%	$40,000	$540,345
2003	28.68%	$40,000	$643,844
2004	10.88%	$40,000	$669,542
2005	4.91%	$40,000	$660,452
2006	15.79%	$40,000	$718,422
2007	5.49%	$40,000	$715,667
2008	-37.00%	$40,000	$425,670
2009	26.46%	$40,000	$487,719
2010	15.06%	$40,000	$515,145
2011	2.11%	$40,000	$485,171
2012	16.00%	$40,000	$516,398
2013	32.39%	$40,000	$630,703
2014	13.69%	$40,000	$671,571
2015	1.38%	$40,000	$640,286
2016	11.96%	$40,000	$672,081
Average	6.16%		

Portfolio 2 Plus Withdrawals			
Year	Market Performance	Annual Withdrawal	Account Balance
2000	2.68%	$40,000	$985,728
2001	0.24%	$40,000	$947,998
2002	-3.14%	$40,000	$879,487
2003	15.78%	$40,000	$971,958
2004	7.68%	$40,000	$1,003,532
2005	3.66%	$40,000	$998,797
2006	8.37%	$40,000	$1,039,049
2007	3.65%	$40,000	$1,035,514
2008	-10.63%	$40,000	$889,691
2009	14.55%	$40,000	$973,321
2010	10.77%	$40,000	$1,033,839
2011	2.00%	$40,000	$1,013,716
2012	13.84%	$40,000	$1,108,478
2013	17.44%	$40,000	$1,254,821
2014	7.03%	$40,000	$1,300,223
2015	-0.42%	$40,000	$1,254,930
2016	9.58%	$40,000	$1,331,320
Average	6.06%		

I believe this is the secret to being successful in retirement. You are willing to give up some upside to avoid the big loss. There is no guarantee you will have returns as in this chart, but by blending a portfolio of assets that have potential for growth with assets that have guarantees, like annuities that generate income, you may have a higher probability of not running out of money in retirement. In retirement, you will want a low-volatility investment discipline.

Inflation

What are we getting from the banks today? Sometimes at the seminars I host, I'll say, "We're getting what, 5, 6 percent?" Depending on the crowd, I might get guffaws or sad and wishful faces in response. In the early 70s and 80s, when we got those 16 percent interest rates, did anyone think there'd be interest rates this low, at 1 percent?

Yet there's almost $9 trillion in cash sitting in the banks.[4] Why? Because they won't give it to us, ba-dum-ching. No. It's there because of the safety. Yet, with the national inflation rate averaging 3 percent, parking your money at the bank means you're losing its value. Inflation has been fairly low in this decade, but we can't rely on that. What if it reaches the crazy highs of the 1980s? If you are only positioned in conservative, low-interest assets, you won't be able to keep up. On the other hand, while market performance historically is the best way to combat the effects of inflation, investing carries a whole set of risks unto itself!

How to address these risks?

---

[4] Federal Reserve Bank of St. Lewis Economic Research. Aug. 31, 2017. "Total Savings Deposits at all Depository Institutions." https://fred.stlouisfed.org/series/WSAVNS.

There is no one-size-fits-all approach, but there is one simple strategy that everyone misses. It's *so* simple you would think everyone's doing it. You'd be wrong. I'm going to throw you a curveball, and a lot of hitters have trouble with the curve.

My wife and I love movies. One of the best ways for us to spend quality time together is snuggled up on the couch watching a favorite movie. One of the "classics" in our house is "Trouble with the Curve," with Clint Eastwood and Amy Adams. It's got a great emotional appeal, and deals with retirement in a lot of ways. It also deals with the fact that baseball has fundamentally changed from its early days. Every few decades, pitchers change their style. As pitchers have upped their game, hitters have changed from fast pitch hits to keeping their eyes out for the tricky pitch. Nothing is trickier than the curve ball—I'm sending you something and it looks like it's coming at you but it's going to curve right to the strike zone and you're going to miss it.

When it comes to getting income in retirement, what you should do is look at having as many SOURCES of income as possible. Many times, you hear people touting the importance of a diversified investment portfolio, but it's equally important to have diversified income sources. If all of your assets are following the same rules in regard to market exposure, tax consequences, inflation, government rules and regulations and so on and so forth, then they will all react the same way. That may be great if we are in a fabulous tax, interest, inflation, legislative, market and legal environment, but how often are all of those things perfectly aligned?

By having multiple sources of income, we can strategically reduce the influence of these possible risks. We want to maximize our income from each and every type of income source we have.

What does that mean?

It means we want to optimize our Social Security checks. We want to be able to make use of the tax-free withdrawals from Roth

IRAs. Instead of living from earnings only from accounts, we develop strategies so we can spend the interest *and* the principal. We should consider guaranteed income streams from an annuity. Are dividends available from life insurance policies? We want to be able to strategically and tax-efficiently take income out of our qualified plans like IRAs and 401(k)s. We want dividends from stocks, rental income from real estate assets, or income from a business you own. We want to be able to explore joint or single life income options on pensions or annuities. In other words, there are a number of income sources you can draw from, and there's no single strategy that is a one-size-fits-all, but do you see how having a variety of sources like those previously listed would be advantageous when it comes to building your retirement paycheck?

Social Security

Much of our income in retirement will likely come from our Social Security check. Yet, for such an important benefit, a lot of people I know feel like they're in the dark when it comes to how to make decisions about their benefits. This is because no one can advise you on taking your Social Security; it's a benefit you earned, and one you have to make decisions for on your own. However, a competent financial advisor can help you see where Social Security fits in the rest of your retirement plan, and will be able to help you figure out which withdrawal strategies match up with your different goals.

There are really three main things that affect your Social Security check:

1. How much you paid in.
2. What your full retirement age (FRA) is.
3. When you start your benefits.

No. 1 is based on your 35 highest earning years. The Social Security Administration uses an indexing formula that involves your anticipated lifespan to decide what a "fair" rate of retirement pay would be when you reach your FRA.

No. 2 is pretty easy to figure out. It used to just be 65 for everyone, but since we all started living longer, the Social Security Administration changed the calculation for FRA to help keep the program solvent. Check out the chart on the following page to see yours.

No. 3 is the one that becomes the most talked about as you near retirement because it's the one that you have the most control over. Most people decide to begin their Social Security checks as soon as the government says they can, typically at 62. Unfortunately, that means they leave a lot of money on the table—we lose 6 percent from our check for every year early that we take Social Security before our FRA. The second-most popular age to take Social Security is 66—the age when most baby boomers reach FRA. At FRA, we qualify for our full benefit. Yet, for the patient, you get about 8 percent MORE in benefits for every year you delay taking your benefits until age 70.[5]

If you're married, you'll want to consider the impact of spousal benefits. A spouse can only get as much as 50 percent of their spouse's benefit at FRA. You don't get an increased benefit for delaying past FRA, nor do you get increased benefits if your spouse delays. Yet, if you or your spouse files before FRA, the early filing can decrease your benefit amount. If you are filing for a spousal benefit, you have to wait for your higher wage-earning spouse to file first. This isn't so if you are filing as a divorced spouse.

---

[5] Emily Brandon. Money, US News. "The Most Popular Ages to Sign Up for Social Security." http://money.usnews.com/money/retirement/articles/2015/06/01/the-most-popular-ages-to-sign-up-for-social-security. Accessed Jan. 5 2017.

Your Full Retirement Age	
Year of Birth	Full Retirement Age
1937 or earlier	65
1938	65 and 2 months
1939	65 and 4 months
1940	65 and 6 months
1941	65 and 8 months
1942	65 and 10 months
1943—1954	66
1955	66 and 2 months
1956	66 and 4 months
1957	66 and 6 months
1958	66 and 8 months
1959	66 and 10 months
1960 or later	67

Social Security planning has a lot to do with what someone has in assets and life expectancy, as well as their personal goals. If we start Social Security too soon for someone who has a long life expectancy, they'll be stuck the rest of their life with a lower check. But what if we started later in life on our Social Security and needed to take more in income from our personal assets to make up the difference? Then we may have drained assets that we were intending to pass on in a legacy—after all, you can't pass on your Social Security benefit. You need to take all those variables into account and arrive at a strategy for drawing Social Security that will optimize Social Security for your own situation.

Integrated Asset Classes

Remember what I said about diversifying asset classes? Let's look at an example of the kind of difference that can make. Let's return to Person A and Person B, who both had a million dollars at retirement.

Person A decided to follow a strategy of withdrawing 5 percent and hopes to maintain their principal throughout life, which may or may not happen. What could go wrong? Market fluctuations, interest rate fluctuations, tax increases, hyperinflation, etc. the list goes on, of course, but we'll keep an optimistic outlook.

Person B, who has the same million dollars, invested the same way, decides they're going to enjoy all of their million dollars over the next 20 years. The big difference here is that Person B, through their working years, had strategically funded a permanent life insurance policy with a death benefit of $1 million.

This is about the presence of having one's life insured in retirement. It's no longer about using life insurance to replace income. It's about using life insurance to protect assets. We'll talk more about this in the protection plan chapter.

As you can see from the following chart, Person B enjoyed more of their assets during their lifetime. After 20 years, their account balance is zero. It appears they have a problem. But, wait a minute. They still have a death benefit guaranteed to last as long as they do. And, at the point that we're 85, 90 years old, mortality has set in and it is possible to see the end of life coming.

I have asked bank loan officers this question: "If an elderly person who was out of money came into your bank and asked if you would loan them $50,000 a year, and the collateral they gave you was a guaranteed life insurance policy, would you make that loan?" The answer I received every time was "Most probably," because they have no risk. In reality, you don't have to go to a bank, because the insurance company will do it for you, guaranteed. And, if a policy such as Person B's is structured properly, the death benefit has grown over time to be much larger than the initial $1 million.

When implementing a concept such as spending principal and earnings over a period of time such as 20 years, make sure you use an advisor who understands the use of life insurance as a tool. There are many types of life insurance and you will want to use a type that is permanent and will last until your death. If using a properly structured and well-funded policy, the death benefit can increase over time and will have a cash value that can act as a source of emergency funds. The death benefit in some policies can also be accessed before death to assist in long-term care or assisted-living expenses. In other words, there are many benefits to using certain features of life insurance in retirement.

Person A vs. Person B				
	Person A		Person B	
Age	Account Balance	Income	Account Balance	Income
65	$1,000,000	$50,000	$1,000,000	$80,243
66	$1,000,000	$50,000	$969,757	$80,243
67	$1,000,000	$50,000	$938,002	$80,243
68	$1,000,000	$50,000	$904,659	$80,243
69	$1,000,000	$50,000	$869,649	$80,243
70	$1,000,000	$50,000	$832,888	$80,243
71	$1,000,000	$50,000	$794,290	$80,243
72	$1,000,000	$50,000	$753,761	$80,243
73	$1,000,000	$50,000	$711,206	$80,243
74	$1,000,000	$50,000	$666,524	$80,243
75	$1,000,000	$50,000	$619,607	$80,243
76	$1,000,000	$50,000	$570,344	$80,243
77	$1,000,000	$50,000	$518,618	$80,243
78	$1,000,000	$50,000	$464,306	$80,243
79	$1,000,000	$50,000	$407,279	$80,243
80	$1,000,000	$50,000	$347,400	$80,243
81	$1,000,000	$50,000	$284,526	$80,243
82	$1,000,000	$50,000	$218,510	$80,243
83	$1,000,000	$50,000	$149,192	$80,243
84	$1,000,000	$50,000	$76,409	$80,243
85	$1,000,000	$50,000	$0	$80,243

Three Income Buckets

One basic way to approach diversity when it comes to your assets is what we call the three-bucket concept.

LIQUID

INCOME

GROWTH

The first bucket is our liquid assets. This is cash, like your bank checking and savings account or CDs. It's for emergencies and opportunities that arise where you might want some money immediately without wanting to worry about tax consequences, withdrawal fees, distribution regulations or consequences to your monthly cash flow.

The second bucket is our income bucket. We take into account Social Security, and pensions if you have one. Bonds would also be placed in this bucket along with some dividend-paying stocks. Annuities are also a source for guaranteed income. This is money we want to be able to count on, so the more that we can have stable and guaranteed, the better. We also want this money to keep pace with inflation so we aren't slipping backward each year in our purchasing power.

The third bucket is our growth bucket. In this bucket, we might have our real estate properties, our stocks and any other market-based products. This bucket is for growing our assets. Because everything in this bucket is subject to market risk, this isn't where we want to be taking our monthly paycheck from. Yet, it also has the most potential for growth, so this is where we look to outstrip inflation (not just keep pace with), and continue to grow our assets both for our own sake and for leaving a legacy if we so choose.

Now, how you have your money split up between these three buckets is really up to you and your goals; I've heard of people who need a very full first bucket just for their own peace of mind. Other people like to have a heavier third bucket, enjoying the potential for returns.

No matter who you are, though, you will want to take a hard look at the second bucket—where is your income coming from?

Freedom in Planning

People usually come to CFG with questions. Questions like:

- Here's my assets, how much can I take in income?
- Or, I have a current amount of money, can I get $100,000 of income from that?
- I have a large portfolio; can I get X income and still have some left over after I die for my family?

They want to plan based upon these questions, not knowing that any plan with that strong of outcomes or mandates will fail. Don't misunderstand—it's not that the person will fail, but that their plan will fail. It's nearly impossible for anything so concrete to work out over multiple decades. We can't predict the future. The problem with these kind of questions is they are a linear way of looking at nonlinear predicaments. Of course, this is pretty typical in the financial services industry.

This linear approach to retirement is what I was originally taught. After 10 years in my career, in October of 1997, I reached a tipping point. I had worked on several retirement income plans for people that I just had very little confidence in. It wasn't that the markets were down or that I was even fearful about a correction at the time. This was 1997, things looked good. There was such a small chance that my clients' income position would still look the same in five years, let alone 20 or 30. Unfortunately, all the other financial professionals I saw around me were planning the same way, linearly, saying "If you have a 5 percent annual return with 3 percent inflation, you'll need to have amassed X amount to take a certain percent income." I was ready to quit the profession altogether. To be clear, I wasn't worried over the retirees themselves; I had a good deal of confidence that they would be fine. I was just dubious about the practicality of their following a plan or strategy that was based on today when I knew very well it might change in the future. This is why we now use modeling software that allows us to run dozens of scenarios about what could happen in the future. It what-ifs everything, and allows you to use a process to mitigate risk.

It comes down to avoiding the linear way of looking at things. To give you another example, let's think about the moon landing in 1969. The computers in our pockets (cellphones) are way more powerful than the computers they used back then. Prior to the moon landing, NASA scientists were using a fairly linear kind of mathematics to get people into orbit around the earth and then safely back. But with the moon landing, it's a different challenge entirely. It's two different destinations. It's three different forces of gravity in action against a tiny capsule in the vacuum of space. It was also a longer journey. With a longer journey, there is more time for things to go wrong. More time for a small miscalculation to become a giant error. More time for unexpected meteorological weather.

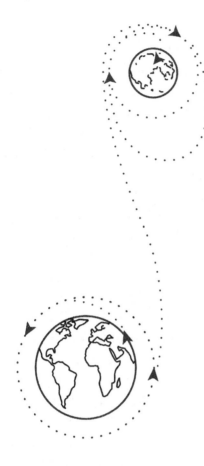

NASA calculates based off of the earth's position, the moon's position, the sun's position, and all their different rotations and movements. Despite all these unknowns and different forces pulling against these celestial bodies—NONE OF IT LINEAR—we used old tech to get the astronauts to the moon AND BACK. How? NASA calculated in "redundancies;" they estimated the ship would need a little more fuel, a little more food, a little more thrust, a little more of everything in case something went wrong, because they knew something would (and did!).

That's the same way we have to approach our finances when we're looking 30 years out.

This expanded, nonlinear approach to income in retirement is in part because you need freedom. Freedom to react to changing circumstances, to take advantage of new opportunities, and to *live* with confidence that your "plans" can change.

I had a client text me at 6:30 a.m. one day. I'm an early riser, and most people know they can get ahold of me sooner in the day rather than later. His text: "Can I see you today?" It must be urgent, right? I texted him back, saying he should meet me for lunch. He responded he knew he was going to have a meeting at work, and he wasn't sure what would happen with his position. He was afraid he'd be let go, or have lots of new job duties loaded on him, and wanted to talk about what his assets would look like if he quit the rat race that day. I knew off the top of my head, because I remembered the modeling, but I knew he wanted the appointment just for the reassurance and confidence for his own sake.

He met me at the office, and I pulled up all his assets, pulled up our modeling software, and we ran through many different scenarios so he could see the various ways things could play out if he retired that day.

When he called me after his meeting with the bosses, he said they had asked him to take on many new responsibilities. Because he had the clarity of purpose and confidence in his financial situation, he had the capability of telling them no. He continued to do the work he wanted, and his bosses let up pressure because he had pushed back in their meeting. Later, he decided to retire when he wanted, on his own terms.

That's the real goal of Your RetireWise Path, is to establish the right process for you to find your financial freedom.

CHAPTER FIVE

RetireWise Tax Plan

W hat do you think of when you think of taxes? You know what I find most people think of? April. Every year, scrambling to get their receipts together for the last year, turning in a pile of paperwork and answering some questions for their accountant so they can file their forms with the IRS.

The problem with this April-focused mentality is that it means we are being reactive about our taxes instead of proactive. But many of the decisions we make in retirement, and in every season of life, have tax implications. We need a better understanding of the impact of taxes on retirement and what some common pitfalls are.

That's why Your RetireWise Path doesn't focus on tax preparation. Instead, we focus on tax *planning*. We focus on identifying opportunities and challenge as they arise. For years, I knew tax planning was important for me and it is just as important for my clients. In our office, as I'm writing this book in late 2017, we're pulling in a strategic alliance with a certified public accountant, or CPA, who can look at our clients' tax situations with this total perspective. I recently bought what was formerly a university's satellite campus building. We're building out a full retirement resource building there, so our CPA will be down the hall instead of across town. It isn't easy, however, to find someone open to true tax planning, someone who is forward thinking. Typically, even our tax professionals think of taxes as a historical event, where we gather our "source documents" and they tell us how much we owe. However, we prefer to work with professionals who understand it is more advantageous to approach taxes by saying in the here and now, "What *should* I be doing to lessen my tax liability in the future?" It's a strategic approach instead of historic.

We like to keep things comfortable and fun, while understanding that we work with the serious topics of people's lives. Yet, in all the time of meeting clients and doing seminars and educational events, I've only had two memorable outbursts from clients or prospective clients. Both times it was about taxes.

A few years ago, one of my associates took me to see his father-in-law. We were discussing how money and taxes work in our economy, and I brought up the opportunity cost of money. Remember, for most of college, I intended to be an accountant. I started talking about opportunity costs, particularly with taxes. The way opportunity costs work is thus: Say you put $500,000 in an investment for 20 years and it compounds at 5 percent every year. If left untouched, it would have grown to about $1.3 million. Sounds great, right? Unfortunately, the earnings are being taxed. Let's say you're in the 25 percent federal tax bracket with a 5 percent state tax. You're probably not using that investment account to pay out those taxes, instead you're taking those from a different "pocket." On top of that, there is a missed opportunity on those tax dollars. If you could have invested the dollars instead of paying a tax, they in turn would have been given the opportunity to grow. For ease of calculation, let's use 5 percent as our rate those dollars could have been invested at. So, your cumulative tax and lost opportunity would be about $400,000. It basically cost you $900,000 ($500,000 principal and about $400,000 lost opportunity to grow your account to $1.3 million. Once you factor in inflation, what $1.3 million is worth 20 years from now, basically, you might just be breaking even. This was a learning moment for the father-in-law and he was not happy about it.

Opportunity Cost of Money: $500,000		
Year	5% Annual Growth	Cumulative Opportunity Cost
1	$525,000	-$7,875
2	$551,250	-$16,538
3	$578,813	-$26,047
4	$607,753	-$36,465
5	$638,141	-$47,860
6	$670,048	-$60,304
7	$703,550	-$73,873
8	$738,728	-$88,647
9	$775,664	-$104,714
10	$814,447	-$122,167
11	$855,170	-$141,103
12	$897,928	-$161,627
13	$942,825	-$183,850
14	$989,966	-$207,893
15	$1,039,464	-$233,879
16	$1,091,437	-$261,945
17	$1,146,009	-$292,233
18	$1,203,310	-$324,894
19	$1,263,475	-$360,091
20	$1,326,649	-$397,995

After I had shared this, and why tax efficiency so important, my associate's father-in-law was MAD. He turned red and hotly said, "Why didn't anyone ever tell me about this? I never thought to calculate this!" I am sure this may be news to you also as you read this.

Here is another tax situation that escapes most everyone, even accountants. In a recent seminar, I asked the audience, "What is the largest asset most retirees hold in retirement?" Someone got it right, their IRA. Then I asked if they knew what happened when they leave the IRA to a surviving spouse after their death? There is usually a loss of income because one of the Social Security incomes is lost and the larger income is kept for the surviving spouse. This loss of income means the spouse will likely need to withdraw more from the IRA, resulting in a higher tax bill. The audience thought this was all that happened. Not so. The surviving spouse is now a single taxpayer, using a different tax table. There is also now only one exemption for the household, and the standard deduction is cut in half, leading to a substantially higher tax bill. One woman stood up, slammed her hand on her table and screamed, "THAT IS WHAT'S HAPPENING TO ME! It's happening to me right now, and no one told me this was coming!" She continued on for a few minutes, yelling about this. It fairly derailed the rest of the seminar, but I understood. She was newly widowed and was faced with losing thousands of dollars every year, she had a right to be mad, didn't she? So did that father-in-law. Hardly anyone talks about these issues, and the consequences are very real.

Goals

Taking a process-driven approach to taxes means that, instead of specific objectives, we have a few overarching goals for learning about and planning ahead for taxes:

- Understand the tax rules we live under.
- Identify misconceptions about taxes in retirement.
- Understand the tools and strategies available to those nearing or in retirement.
- Avoid the political and stick to the actionable.

Income Taxes

Income taxes were originally supposed to be temporary, some Congresses had ushered in various income taxes during wartime, but in 1913 the federal government first began what was a temporary income tax that become the very permanent income tax.

Locally we have a similar experience. In Topeka, voters elected to implement a quarter-cent sales tax in 1995, only to see it raised to a half-cent in 2004, and a recent extension holds that "temporary" tax in place until 2033. Temporary, like the income tax.[6]

The fluctuating nature of income taxes can seem disconcerting, until you realize that, nationally, we once had a 90 percent tax rate. Did you know that? Apparently, President Ronald Reagan told White House staff that, back in his movie-making days, he wasn't interested in making more than two movies a year because, after a certain point, he only got to keep 10–30 percent of his paycheck.[7]

Take a look at the chart and you'll see we're actually in a relatively low tax environment. When we're talking about your marginal tax rate, we're talking about the tax rate you're spending on your last dollar of income. So, if you are in a 45 percent marginal tax rate, that doesn't mean you're paying 45 percent on ALL of your income.

[6] Tim Hrenchir. Topeka Capital-Journal. June 3, 2004. "County Approves Adding Tax Question to Ballot." http://cjonline.com/stories/060304/bre_county.shtml#.WbL808j5iUk.

Aly Van Dyke. Topeka Capital-Journal. Nov. 4, 2014. "Voters approve 15-year extension of half-cent sales tax." http://cjonline.com/news-local/2014-11-04/voters-approve-15-year-extension-half-cent-sales-tax.

[7] Deborah Hart Strober and Gerald Strober. Houghton Mifflin. June 30, 1998. "Reagan: The Man and His Presidency."

U.S. Historical Marginal Tax Rates

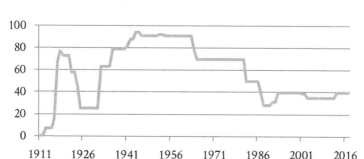

Do you think our taxes are likely to go down? Let me ask this a different way—do you know what the U.S. national debt is? There's a website dedicated just to tracking our debt, www.usdebtclock.org, and we're close to topping $20 trillion as I write this in fall 2017. According to the site, current revenue per taxpayer is about $28,000, but the debt per taxpayer is about $166,000. So, back to the main question, do you think our tax rate will go down?

The best lesson I learned from tax planning was from my dad. In the 80s and early 90s, the overall tax rates were at their lowest. My dad retired in 1986. Instead of taking income from his pension and retirement savings, he took a lump sum of his pension and paid the taxes on all his retirement assets, because the highest tax rate that year was 28 percent, and he remembered how uncertain taxes could be and wanted to minimize his exposure.

He knew, you're almost always going to pay taxes, but when often determines how much.

Vocabulary on "tax breaks"

We talk a lot about taking advantage of "tax breaks" and "loopholes," but basically there are three things we to talk about when it comes to the "line items" of taxes.

Credits are designed to incentivize behavior. They are the government's way of pushing us to do something. We've got the health care tax credit, the earned income tax credit, education credits, savers credits, etc. It's like a little tax gift from Uncle Sam for doing well that you can use to offset a tax liability.

Deductions are the things you spent money on that reduced your taxable income. There's the "standard" deduction, which for 2017 is $12,700 for married couples or $6,350 for single people. There are also "itemized" deductions, such as donations to charities, mortgage interest and property taxes or business expenses for a personal side business. Those over 65 or those who are blind have additional deductions.

Exemptions are a reduction to your income for the necessary expenses of living for whoever you claim as a dependent. For tax year 2017, that amount is $4,050 per person in your household.

These are important to understand particularly because of how they interplay with debt. People come into CFG getting ready to retire, and they want to pay off their home. The idea of going into retirement with debt of any kind scares them. While I'm a fan of living debt free, people need to consider the total situation before making a snap decision. For one thing, a mortgage may be a debt, but it has a lot of safety—locked-in rates, refinancing options that can stretch the amortization schedule... Many people want to cash in part of their IRA to pay off their home. But they haven't realized this can become a twofold problem. For one thing, cashing in on IRA assets has tax consequences and, especially when someone takes it in a lump sum like that, they are susceptible to being pushed into a higher tax bracket (which, of course, means they'll have to withdraw even more than what they owe on their mortgage so they'll have enough left over to pay taxes). Plus, they will lose their mortgage tax deduction. Emotionally, it might feel good to have no mortgage, but realistically, I hear "WHAT DID I DO?" because of the taxes.

401(k) and IRA

Many of us have been saving in tax-deferred accounts like 401(k)s and IRAs. Tax-deferred isn't tax-free; at some point the government is going to want its tax money. You will pay income tax on all of your withdrawals from these accounts. While many people think this isn't a big deal and that they'll be in a lower tax bracket in retirement, think about it. What will your lifestyle be? What did you determine in Your RetireWise Path income step? Do you plan to have less income in retirement? And don't forget our discussion about being widowed in retirement and what happens to us with the taxes on these accounts.

RMDs

If you don't make withdrawals from your tax-deferred accounts, don't think you are getting around those tax laws; like I said, the government will get its tax money. So, there are required minimum distributions, or RMDs, you legally must begin withdrawing by age 70 ½, or you'll pay 50 percent penalty on taxes on whatever your RMD was *supposed* to be. Your RMD is calculated based off of your anticipated life expectancy and your account's ending balance the previous year.

Social Security

Are you surprised to see Social Security on the list of tax considerations? Some people I talk to are surprised to find that their Social Security is taxable. Your benefits are taxed based on the provisional income formula.

Your provisional income is your adjusted gross income, plus any tax-free interest, plus 50 percent of your Social Security benefits. If you are single and your total is less than $25,000, or you are married and the total is less than $32,000, your benefits are tax-free. If your provisional income is between $25,000 and $34,000 for a single person and $32,000 and $44,000 for married couples, 50 percent of your benefits are taxed. If your provisional income is more than $34,000 for a single person and $44,000 for a married couple, up to 85 percent of benefits will be subject to taxes. These thresholds have remained constant the past years.

Taxes on High Net Worth Individuals

Net Investment Income Tax

In 2013, tax laws changed to include a net investment income tax. Basically, this means the government will take an additional 3.8 percent tax on the lesser of:

- Adjusted gross income above $250,000 for married couples or $200,000 for single filers

OR

- Net investment income (capital gains + dividends plus interest + annuity payments + passive business income + rental income etc.)

PEP

The Personal Exemption Phaseout reduces your allowed personal exemption by 2 percent for every $2,500 of income that you have in excess of $261,500 for single people and $313,800 for married couples.

Pease Limitation

Named for Rep. Donald Pease, the Pease Limitation reduces a filer's itemized deductions by 3 percent of the amount of their adjusted gross income over $261,500 for single people and $313,800 for married couples. It can take away up to 80 percent of the value of your itemized deductions, but doesn't apply to medical, invest-ment interest, casualty and theft and gambling loss deductions.

Alternative Minimum Tax

An alternative minimum tax is conceptually simple—the IRS levies a flat tax of 26-28 percent of a person's income over a rela-tively high threshold. You are required to pay whichever is higher—the alternative minimum tax or your regular income tax. The diffi-culty is in calculating the alternative minimum tax, since you have to start with your 1040 adjusted gross income and work backward, adding in deductions and adjusting for transactions that are treated differently for the alternative minimum tax than regular income tax. To see what I mean, you can check out the list of different items considered in your AMT qualification on the IRS website: https://apps.irs.gov/app/amt2016/assistant/process?execu-tion=e1s1.

Capital Gains

Public policy on capital gains—the gains you make on invest-ments—and qualified dividends is meant to encourage investors to keep their money in the market. This is the primary explanation for why long-term capital gains and dividends brackets are so far from what income tax brackets look like.

Marginal Tax Bracket	Long-Term Capital Gains
10%	0%
15%	0%
25%	15%
28%	15%
33%	15%
35%	15%
39.6%	20%

Of course, short-term capital gains—gains from assets you both bought and sold within a year and a day—are taxed at the same rate as ordinary income tax

---

Strategies

So, with all of these taxes just waiting to take a bite, how can you position your assets to be efficient and to avoid overpaying taxes? Following are some approaches that can help you mitigate your tax exposure, which we routinely work with tax professionals to help plan for and implement. They're all, of course, general; the strategy you use will depend on your own personal situation and goals, but the overarching theme of tax planning is to diversify your income sources. It doesn't help to put your eggs in one basket if that basket's rules are subject to change!

Tax Buckets

In my seminars, I often ask couples about their shopping habits. In the last event we did, I picked on two couples. The first couple started laughing—the wife said she very consciously chooses products based on her objectives, their quality and price. She said if she were to send her husband to the store, she would end up with a cart full of unrelated ingredients they may or may not even need. The other couple smiled nervously at each other. The wife admitted they frequently do the shopping together, because she tends to overspend and impulse-buy while her husband carefully questions each purchase.

Unfortunately, when we're in the accumulation phase of our lives, when we're acquiring our assets, we all tend to be the willy-nilly shopper—saving money where we can, but not necessarily thinking through each decision carefully. After all, we're caught up in the rat race—who has time to make those plans? Isn't it enough to just save in the first place? Really, this isn't the worst attitude; it really is better to save than to not, period. But, once we're looking to deal with taxes and be efficient, we have to change our thinking.

One of the easiest ways we have discovered at CFG to help people shift that thinking is through buckets. We obviously like buckets—remember the income buckets in the last chapter? Well, these are different buckets. They're your tax buckets.

TAXABLE

The first bucket is our taxable bucket. Our savings and CDs, stocks, bonds and mutual funds are here. These are the assets where you paid taxes on the principal and which the IRS evaluates annually to see if you owe taxes on your gains.

TAX-DEFERRED

The second bucket is our tax-deferred bucket. Your 401(k), IRA, 403(b) and some others are in this bucket. You didn't pay tax on the principal here, so instead you will pay income taxes on everything that comes out of this bucket, whether it's in the form of a conversion or income withdrawals.

TAX-FREE

The third bucket, and possibly my favorite, is the tax-free bucket. Your Roth 401(k) and Roth IRA are here, as well as life insurance assets. You paid taxes on the front end of these assets, before you made a purchase, so they are now largely outside of tax considerations.

If we thought income taxes were going to increase in the future, where would you want your assets to be? Most people would say "I'd like to end up in a tax-free bucket."

I agree. Over a period of time, we'd like to think strategically, how could we move toward that tax-free bucket? I say "strategically," because we probably wouldn't like it to happen all at one time. So, one idea of the tax bucket system is to move assets toward a tax-free position.

Not to harp too hard on a central theme, but one of the best ways to skip the rat race when it comes to taxes is to use the tools you have to diversify among account types and to make sure that what you have in each bucket makes sense there—and that you're withdrawing income strategically from each of them.

Roth Conversion

One strategy you can employ for 401(k)s and IRAs is to strategically convert your funds from a traditional tax-deferred account to a Roth account. Let me be clear: you will pay the taxes on the funds that come from the traditional account before they go into a Roth account. This is one reason that I stress the word "strategic": you don't want to convert a sizeable IRA asset all at once lest the withdrawals be counted as regular income and push you into a higher tax bracket for that year.

Filling Brackets

When it comes to moving assets from one account to another, one of the ways you can strategically avoid paying more in income taxes is what we call "filling up the bracket." For instance, let's say you're looking to avoid taking RMDs in retirement on a sizeable IRA. For 2017, let's say your taxable income is $175,000, putting you in the 28 percent tax bracket. If you're married filing jointly, that means you have $58,350 of additional income you could earn before getting pushed up into the 33 percent tax bracket. So, for that year, you would convert $58,350 of your traditional IRA to a Roth. This strategic movement does require time and planning ahead, but it can be a helpful way to both avoid paying an unusually high tax bill while also reducing your future tax liability.

Putting it all together

For an example, let's look at a couple who is approaching 70 ½. Looking into the future, they know they will likely not leave this world at the same time, as I wrote about earlier in this chapter. They know a likely scenario is one of them will pass away, and whoever remains may have similar expenses to married life—they will still need to pay for the home, groceries, travel expenses, transportation, entertainment, etc. However, the survivor will have lost the lower Social Security benefit, and will be counted as a single taxpayer now. Whomever is left will likely be in a position to pull more from their as-of-yet untaxed IRA to make up the difference in income. Even if they have many years left together, they are approaching 70 ½ and must pull RMDs from their IRA. So, they smartly consider some ways to lessen that tax impact.

They would be well situated to moving toward a tax-free environment, meaning that they will perhaps convert their IRA to a Roth or use it to purchase life insurance. Whatever strategy they want to use, we'll want to start repositioning them in the tax-free bucket sooner than later.

CAUTION: The Sky Is Not Falling

Particularly when it comes to taxes, although I'm a big proponent of what-iffing everything and stress-testing, I'd like to bring a dose of levity. You should hope for the best and prepare for the worst, but don't *panic.* Particularly in financial services, there are always people who encourage a worst-case-scenario mentality and take advantage of people's worries. Just like panic can push us to make poor investing decisions, the same can happen with tax positions.

I had a man come into my office who had been watching a lot of TV, and became so convinced by a slick sales commercial such a massive tax hike was coming and the dollar would become worthless that he cashed in his entire IRA to buy gold. Thankfully, he was in a 60-day return window. He went back and was able to have the supplier reverse the sale, and the IRS allowed it, no harm no foul.

It must have been a terribly effective commercial to instill that level of panic in this man, but I think this story illustrates the dangers of indulging our feelings too much instead of using logic and reason to make important financial decisions. We never want to be sitting there as Chicken Little, screaming the sky is falling.

Importance of Planning

A lot of us approach retirement with this idea of defer, defer, defer. We intend to defer taxes indefinitely. But the way tax deferral works is that you will pay now or you will pay later; there's not a "never" setting.

I'd like to pay special attention to the example I used when it comes to widows and widowers. We are not gifted with immortality. The single largest asset most people have is an IRA or its equivalent, which they intend to leave to their surviving spouse. Everyone has good intentions but, in reality, this sort of planning sets us up for a triple income whammy.

1. The surviving spouse loses a Social Security check.
2. The surviving spouse usually turns to assets like an IRA to make up the difference in income, which means paying taxes for the first time on these assets.
3. The big one → The surviving spouse will now be filing as a SINGLE person. They will no longer have the break of a joint status, and will climb up those marginal brackets.

This is something I find most people are not planning for. I've had CPAs who don't talk about it. Yet this is one of those key reasons that preparing early and having a process for approaching taxes is so crucial in retirement.

I'd like to point out: throughout this chapter we've used the most current tax tables we have available to us as of this writing at the end of 2017. They may look very different in the coming years as different administrations have their hands at the tiller, consequently affecting the tax strategies we've listed here. However, the overarching point that is important to remember on taxes is to be proactive, always looking ahead instead of being pushed into a corner and feeling forced into a tax reaction.

CHAPTER SIX

RetireWise Protection

How confident are you that you have done everything possible to be sure failure is not an option for your retirement? One key piece of Your RetireWise Path is about protecting what we have. Prudent investing, a pragmatic income plan and even a prepared approach to taxes isn't enough if all of these plans don't also include the element of a well-thought-out protection plan.

When I think of protection, I think of you and your assets as a castle with a moat, like in medieval times. Old grand castles had moats for protection, complete with sludge, and contingencies to thwart whatever invaders and enemies came their way. What does your moat look like; how well protected are you? I often ask the question, "If you could buy insurance after a catastrophic event occurred, how much would you buy?" The answer I would get is "As much as I could get." Well, of course an insurance company will not do that, and there is a limit to how much they will issue to insure your assets, income or life. It is up to the replacement value. The reason most people don't carry adequate coverage is the perceived cost. When planning for my clients, the principle is full protection at minimum cost. This takes some work and writing notes for my clients to take to their insurance agents to make corrections. We usually handle the life insurance because of the multiple benefits it provides as you will see later in this chapter.

Our castle and its moat should have no cracks and no chance of failure. This is even more important in retirement than in our working life because, once you've withdrawn from the workforce, you no longer have an income to replace any assets you may lose in the case of an unfortunate event. We can't predict the future, of course, but we can protect those things that are critical to supporting our dreams in retirement:

- Assets
- Income
- Life

Current assets

Much of our current financial situation is largely dependent on our assets. Our lifestyle, our future income and, in many ways, our health are all dependent on our assets and our ability to reposition them accordingly. So, how do we protect our castle and keep it from crumbling?

Well, protection for our assets is based on well-structured property and casualty insurance. Insurance is in place to replace and protect the value of something. If my home burns down, do I want just part of it replaced or all of it? All of it. The biggest gap in most people's protection plan, though, is their liability limits are too low. The biggest risk all of us have is a liability claim because we injured someone in our vehicle or they were hurt on our premises. Those losses can easily exceed the loss of an asset, but they don't always reach the paper. We're all familiar with the necessity of car insurance, and the fact that you must have some level of it to be allowed to drive. However, few people realize that most states' mandatory level of minimum insurance is well below the financial liability you will face if you injure someone with your vehicle.

It may seem like a small thing, but basic insurance can be a big deal. Lawsuits over dog bites or rental properties or car accidents have ruined more than one robust savings account. So, do yourself a favor and what-if your basic coverage. My suggestion to most all my clients is to carry a liability umbrella that gives extra protection over the base policies of auto and homeowners policies. The minimum is usually $1,000,000 in coverage and the premiums are very low, around $150 to $200 in annual premium.

Income

While we're working, we usually pick up at least a minimum level of disability insurance through work. Some of us may have picked up a policy outside of work, as well, to be sure we have enough coverage to preserve some income to be able to make basic expenses while we are unable to work.

A disability in retirement means we need assistance when we become unable to do the activities of daily life. When we are unable to do two or more activities such as toileting, bathing, eating, dressing or grooming ourselves unassisted, we need long-term care of some sort, such as assisted living, in-home care or nursing home care.

It's easy to hear people discount the idea of needing long-term care. Yet, according to LongTermCare.gov, 70 percent of those 65 and older *will* need some kind of long-term care. Seven out of 10. Remember that plane analogy? I asked if you'd get off the plane if it only had a 90 percent chance of landing safely. What about if it had a 70 percent chance of NOT landing safely? Yet, people often don't prepare for this cost. My wife and I experienced this with our parents, who have all passed on now. Three out of four of our parents required assistance.

For one thing, they incorrectly assume the government will step in. They're right that Medicaid will step in…eventually. But only after you have exhausted your own resources to the point of poverty. Most of us would agree that's not the ideal scenario, right?

Part of the difficulty is in the tools we have available at our disposal for preparing for long-term care. Perhaps the most straightforward is long-term-care insurance. Unfortunately, long-term-care insurance has a few drawbacks that make it unattractive:

1. Premiums are increasingly expensive the older you are.
2. If you know you will likely need it, in other words, if you have already begun to lose your health, you can't get it.
3. Modern contracts' premiums aren't guaranteed—most contracts issued today are "guaranteed renewable," meaning your benefits are guaranteed to renew year to year, but the cost of the policy may increase. The insurance company can

file with the state at any given time to raise premiums if they discover their policies are losing ground.

4. It's a use-it-or-lose-it proposition—if you die without ever needing long-term care, you will not have the value of the policy or anything equivalent to pass on.

Again, seven out of 10 of us will need long-term care of some kind, but a lot of people still wonder, "What if I'm one of those other three? Do I want to pay into a policy for years that I never use?" For some people, long-term-care insurance can really make sense and be a foundational piece of their protection planning. For others, we may want to come up with other funding options.

For one thing, we might try to help them "self-fund." In Kansas, the cost of a semi-private room at a nursing home in 2016 was $5,201 a month. At-home services were $3,813 a month. Self-funding entails looking at that range of costs and setting aside a certain amount of assets to pay for around three years' worth of care. What makes this extra tricky is that it's difficult to calculate *future* costs of care, since inflation notoriously affects health and long-term care differently than other areas of the economy. Also, married couples may need twice as much—what if both spouses are incapacitated and need long-term care?[8]

The following chart illustrates what the total cost of care might be for a couple at differing levels of care. What if she doesn't need care, but he needs home care? Or, what if both of them need facilitative care? If you look at the chart, you can see, $576,000 a year is no laughing matter.

---

[8] Genworth. 2016. "Genworth Cost of Care Survey 2016." https://www.genworth.com/about-us/industry-expertise/cost-of-care.html.

Considering Long-Term Care Costs for Two				
		If She Needs...		
		No Care	*Home or Assisted Care*	*Facilitative Care*
If He Needs...	*No Care*	$0	$144,000	$288,000
	Home or Assisted Care	$144,000	$288,000	$432,000
	Facilitative Care	$288,000	$432,000	$576,000

Another source to help with the expense of long-term care is to use an annuity that includes guaranteed income but also includes a benefit that will double the contract holder's income for up to five years if one is unable to perform two of six activities of daily living, and then reverts back to the income payment.

People like this funding style partly because, if they never need long-term care, they will still receive the income benefit of the annuity. The guaranteed income or withdrawal benefit can perform double-duty for us by having the income double when assistance is needed. There are many variations to the benefit, depending on the annuity product issued by the insurance company.

You have to be careful in your search for products that will accomplish this, of course, and work with a professional who can help you make sure they are structured properly. Also, remember that annuities are backed by the claims-paying ability of the issuing insurance company.

A big piece of protecting your future income is about health care, even aside from long-term care. If you are one of those three lucky people out of 10 who never need in-home services or other long-term health care, you will still need basic health care in retirement.

Unfortunately, while many people think it will just all be taken care of by Medicare, this is just totally inaccurate. Several different companies have studied and surveyed retirees over the course of retirement, and the general consensus is that a healthy couple retiring at 65 will spend a ballpark of $250,000 in retirement *on Medicare premiums alone.*[9]

Those costs are only expected to climb as inflation takes its toll, and they don't account for all of the other expenses like dental and vision care that aren't covered by Medicare.

We have no idea what might happen tomorrow when it comes to health care, do we? Is the Affordable Care Act/Obamacare going to be repealed? Replaced? Is Medicare going to expand or retract?

We know health care is going to change, but we don't know how it will change. Currently, it's a chore just to be familiar with the alphabet soup of Medicare coverage options.

So, examine your Medicare options with a financial professional, and be sure that you have thoroughly considered your wraparound insurance coverage options.

---

[9] Katie Lobosco. CNN Money. Dec. 30, 2015. "Don't freak out about health care costs in retirement." http://money.cnn.com/2015/12/30/retirement/retirement-health-care-costs/index.html.

Alphabet of Medicare Coverage[10]

	Basics	Coverage	Cost (2017)
Part A	Original Medicare. Part A benefits are a federal benefit.	Major medical/ disaster coverage.	Free for most, though the highest premium is $413/mo, plus a $1,316 deductible for hospital stays.
Part B	Near-essential wrap-around coverage for Part A, a federal benefit you can enroll in for a premium.	Doctor's visits, preventative care, diagnostics and medical equipment.	$183 deductible, plus 20% of all costs after that with no limit on out-of-pocket expenses
Part C	Called "Medicare Advantage," a private insurance alternative to Part A and B.	Parts of Part A and B, varies by insurance carrier.	Premiums subject to coverage and insurer
Part D	Supplemental coverage through private insurers, primarily for prescriptions.	Prescriptions	Varies by carrier and coverage. Many plans don't begin coverage until you've spent $3,700 out-of-pocket on prescriptions, called the "donut hole" of coverage.
Med-Sup	Also known as Medigap, or with names like "Part F" this is private insurance meant to pick up the tab for whatever Medicare A-D won't.	Varies by carrier and coverage.	Varies by carrier and coverage.

---

[10] Medicare. 2017. "Your Medicare Costs." https://www.medicare.gov/your-medicare-costs/.

Life

The last piece of protection we really should focus on is your life. This has a double meaning. It partly means we should be sure all of our protection process is geared to protect in case of longevity, but it also means we should be protecting our assets as part of our legacy in case we don't get that longevity.

Remember the two people we named Person A and Person B in the chapter on income? What made Person B's greater income plan was the presence of a permanent death benefit in retirement. Most other financial professionals miss that protection in the plan. They assume you carry life insurance in your working years just to replace income for your loved ones in case you die. They assume that, when you retire, you don't have a need for the insurance. What happens with a well-structured plan is that life insurance now starts to protect assets that we want to use for income. It is the presence of a permanent death benefit that allows the most powerful income strategies.

Brother B had a permanent death benefit, which protected $1,000,000 in assets used for income. The death benefit allowed Person B to spend both earnings and principal because the death benefit would replace other assets. This allows him the protection of not having to pursue high rates of return. In turn, he may take less risk with his money and is less susceptible to interest rate risk and tax risk. Even if Person B runs out of money at an older age— say 85 or so—mortality will have set in. At an older age, Person B can strategically use his death benefit to provide income.

Now, I want to be clear that this isn't a "strategy" in and of itself— any planning of this kind should only be done in conjunction with a knowledgeable and experienced financial advisor. Yet, I think it's a powerful concept, the ability to unlock your assets and use them in their entirety the way you want. For Person B, even if they die prematurely, their spouse is protected for income by the death benefit replacing the assets. You can look at it this way. We are coordinating guaranteed benefits with a guaranteed event.

Another protection element of life insurance with newer policies is the ability to use life insurance to help provide some long-term-care benefits. A portion of the life insurance death benefit can be used to pay for the cost of long-term care. This makes a lot of sense because now you have coverage you know is going to pay a benefit, whether it is for critical care or a death benefit. This helps fill a very big hole in most people's retirement plans.

About 20 years ago, I was at a forum at Hotel del Coronado in California. It was an event for financial professionals, and one of the speakers was a Southern Baptist preacher whose son, one of our fellow advisors, had recently died. It seemed like a curious choice at first, but I'll never forget what he said: "I learned from my son that you are not ready to live until you are ready to die." His son had, earlier in his life, very deliberately structured a financial plan to take care of the people he loved, and also maintained a steady relationship with his Creator. After doing this, the man said, his son lived fully, taking risks and going where God wanted him to go. He was liberated to live as he felt called, because he was ready for the alternative.

This struck me because of both its financial and spiritual implications for our lives. Financially, when you have developed a well-thought-out protection plan that includes your assets, your income and life, you are much freer to live and enjoy life than when you are living with a cloud of what-ifs and questions.

If you could write your will from the grave, what would you want it to say? What might you have done differently? It's key, of course, to work with a competent estate planning attorney who can help you understand ways to protect your assets in case of death or an extreme health event to be sure assets aren't lost or confiscated.

One of the most important things married couples can do is consider their estate planning strategies. We often romantically think of what we want to happen to our joint assets as though we will exit life on the same day. Yet, a spouse may be widowed for decades. It's important to consider how to protect your spouse in scenarios such as the loss of Social Security income and increased taxes.

I don't often "fire" clients or prospective clients. I pride myself in being able to meet people where they're at and help them. However, one couple comes to mind when it comes to the importance of protecting a spouse. This couple sat down with me after purchasing a sizeable new home in retirement. As we reviewed their plans and assets, I looked at this new house and their protection plans. The way they were structured, if he died early, her life would change in a big way. She would have to move out of the home, away from new neighbors who became friends, and start over in retirement.

As we discussed this, it became very clear: The prospect of moving after her husband's death terrified her, but he didn't take it very seriously. It was an easy fix by insuring the husband in this case, which they could afford to do, but he didn't want to. I didn't want to work with this couple after that. I couldn't in good conscience continue to execute plans that were so obviously to the detriment of the future needs of one spouse, and had no desire to work with someone who didn't seem to care about the possible future impacts of his decisions on his spouse.

Your RetireWise Path is built to weave protection in around all the other pieces of your plan, to be sure that it's protecting your assets, income and life, as well as protecting you from inflation, taxes and things of that nature. Using protection as part of your process keeps your plans more stable. I remember in college in the late 70s, my wife wanted to go visit her brother in California. We geared up for the big weekend trip, and just as we were ready to leave, the oil embargo really hit home. Before leaving for California, I heard the lines at the pumps were two miles long. As a college kid, I recognized it immediately: This was a change of plans! Yet, we know that things like hyperinflation or unexpected costs do more than stall out a trip west once we're in retirement. That's why it's best to build protection into your process.

I see it as similar to chess. Your world-class master chess players think strategically. Chess is a game of strategy. When they think through moves, they are thinking "what's the best offensive move, what's the best defensive move" at the same time.

For football fans, perhaps a different analogy is more effective. When Super Bowl time comes around, everyone has a prediction about who's going to win. My guess is always based on who has the best defensive team. The team with the best defense usually wins. In 2008 and 2012, New England and the New York Giants played. I chose the Giants both times because they had a stronger defense and they won, twice. When Seattle played the Broncos, everyone thought the Broncos would CRUSH them, right? They were wrong. Seattle had the better defense. If you want to win in the retirement game, you have to have a strong defense. You want the maximum protection benefits at the minimum cost, you want to be sure there are no cracks in your plan. If there are cracks, there is a chance for failure. You want full protection.

CHAPTER SEVEN

RetireWise Legacy and Estate Plan

What is the legacy you intend to leave behind? I'm not just talking about money. That's certainly a consideration, but, while not everyone leaves money when they depart this world, everyone leaves a legacy.

You probably think this chapter is about having a trust, avoiding estate tax, etc. All those things are important, but they are easily done if you are motivated to do them. Yet, what motivates most people is the relationship they have with their children, friends, community, etc. We're going to focus on that. The rest is easy to put together when you focus on why. Values clear, decisions easy.

Our mission at CFG is "Building Wealth That Lasts." When we hear the word wealth, most people gravitate toward material riches. But the word should conjure up more in our minds. I know of a number of people who do not possess the "world's treasures," but would be considered wealthy. The following illustration is how I think of wealth.

Wealth that Lasts

I would like to share my thinking on wealth. If we have saved or built wealth, whether it be financial, relational or wisdom assets, we don't want to lose them. As a matter of fact, we would like to pass them on to our children or grandchildren; in other words, we'd like to make it generational. How we approach and handle wealth also has an eternal element. Allow me to quote Jesus. In the Bible, Mathew 6:19-21, He says, "Do not lay up for yourselves treasures on earth, where moth and rust destroy and where thieves break in and steal; but lay up for yourselves treasures in heaven, where neither moth nor rust destroys and where thieves do not break in and steal. For where your treasure is, there your heart will be also." Let us not forget this most significant and meaningful wealth. How we handle this world's wealth has an impact on eternal wealth.

WEALTH THAT LASTS

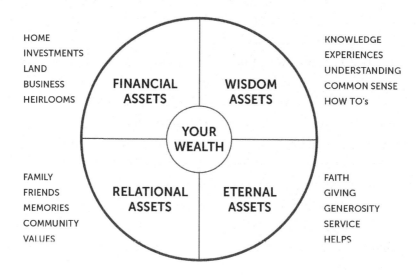

On the fourth Friday of every month, my wife and I invite new clients into our home for dinner and casual conversation. Typically, these clients don't know each other prior to the dinner, but it's amazing how they communicate with each other about this important event in their life—retirement—because it's what they have in common. Sometimes it takes a little bit to get them talking, but with the influence of this shared experience—and more than a little of Sheryl's delicious cooking—the conversation is soon flowing fast and free. After they've started their conversations, I often ask, "What do you want your children or those close to you to receive from you after you've passed on?" What I hear from them is not so much about the financial things, even though all of them will be leaving financial things. What I do hear is this:

- "I want them to share my faith."
- "I want them to have memories."
- "I want them to tell the children who I was."
- "I want them to have amazing life experiences."
- "I want them to have the stories of our heritage."

So, although I want to talk about things like estate planning and wills and trusts, I'd like to start by talking about your *real* legacy.

Your Circle

I'm a reader by nature, and I keep a journal of my thoughts, meditations and the things that I've read that have given me a mental nudge. One of the books that makes frequent appearances in my journal, particularly when it comes to legacy, is the book "Letters from Dad," by Greg Vaughn. The author's father died after a battle with Alzheimer's disease, leaving many things left unsaid and undone. After, the only significant thing Vaughn had left from his father was a tackle box with lures. His grief turned to anger, which eventually became a self-reflection: What was it he wanted his children to know, in the event of his demise? The premise of the book was that it's important to tell the people you care about what is important for them to know while you still have the chance. If everyone leaves a legacy, wouldn't you rather choose what yours would be?

One movie that I think makes a point—however comically—about family and legacy is "Meet the Parents," with Ben Stiller and Robert DeNiro. DeNiro plays a former CIA operative whose daughter is in a serious realationship with Stiller. During the course of the movie, Stiller's character can't seem to do anything right. From destroying prized family possessions to ruining secrets and injuring people, he brings a comedy of errors, all while trying to impress DeNiro and join "the circle of trust." DeNiro, of course, is big on trust, and in both the original and the sequel, he continues to harangue Stiller about his inclusion—or non-inclusion—in the circle of trust. As slapstick-hilarious as the movie is, it begs the very serious question of who is in your circle?

In our family, we have made a habit of writing notes and letters to our children and grandchildren, to communicate within our circle of trust. Another family tradition of ours is the idea of vacations with a purpose. I intentionally started taking my whole family—wife, kids, grandkids—on vacation, all at once, so we can spend time one-on-one and as a whole. This way we can communicate our values to not only our children, but their children, and instill in them a sense of purpose.

Another book that has impacted my idea of legacy is "The Blessing" by John Trent and Gary Smalley. Much of what it focuses on is how to impart blessings to your children, how to communicate the things that will affirm their character. It centers on the Old Testament traditions of giving and receiving blessings. When it comes to planning a legacy, I think this idea is incredibly impactful because, while our clients may have certain intentions, we also suggest that they bring their children and family members together to discuss the intentions behind these gifts, and to talk about how to receive them.

Why is that important? I'm a Proverbs reader, so I think of Proverbs 20:21—"An inheritance gained hastily at the beginning will not be blessed at the end."

In practical application, we see this truth in the observation that numerous adult children have no idea how to handle wealth. Some retirees don't intend to leave an inheritance behind to future generations because they're certain it would be squandered. To me, that sounds as though there isn't just a problem with the children, but with the way the parents communicated how to handle things of value. For our part, Sheryl and I are very proud of our sons and what they have accomplished in their lives. I would trust them all with anything. I can't take all the credit for that, but there are a few foundational disciplines when it comes to money and value that can help hold people accountable, not to mention practical steps such as a properly structured estate plan.

About 13 years ago, I was at a conference that the presenter was sharing excerpts from his book "Missed Fortune." One was a retelling of families who amassed wealth, only to see it squandered in a matter of decades. Specifically, the story of the Vanderbilts and the Rothschilds stuck with me.

Vanderbilts

All students of U.S. history should recognize Cornelius Vanderbilt (1794-1877), the 1800s entrepreneur. He was the most successful businessman of his time, a steamship and railroad magnate who profited as Westward Expansion became the frontier of progress. He was not known for being charitable, but a $1 million donation to what would become Vanderbilt University secured part of his vast legacy. And the $150 million he left to his family upon his death in 1877?

Arthur T. Vanderbilt II detailed in his own book, "Fortune's Children: The Fall of the House of Vanderbilt," that in 1973, 120 of Cornelius' descendants reunited, and there was not a single millionaire amongst them. Cornelius' grandson, William K. Vanderbilt, lamented, "It has left me with nothing to hope for, with nothing definite to seek or strive for. Inherited wealth is a real handicap to happiness."

Rothschilds

Mayer Amschel Rothschild (1743-1812) was a banker in Frankfurt, Germany, who brought his sons into business, teaching them his conservative money management style. They invested on behalf of socialites and royalty, focusing on profits that were reasonable and stable rather than riskier and aggressive. They made a tremendous fortune, and branched out to found other banks across Europe. Though you may not have heard of this family—they eschew the limelight—they reputedly have maintained and even diversified their fortune, holding stakes in industries from small farming to energy to art to nonprofits. The family still controls the Rothschild banks that bear their name.

So, how can it be that two men who were the final word in business, so to speak, have such different outcomes in their families' fortunes?

The Rothschild family founder thought ahead. In addition to meticulously attending to his sons' financial education, he developed principals of money management that he made institutional within the family, running it much like a corporate entity in and of itself.

"Basically, the Rothschilds established the following system:

- They loaned their heirs money or entered into joint ventures with them.
- The loans had to be paid back to the 'family bank.'
- The knowledge and experiences those heirs gained had to be shared with other family members.
- The family gathered at least once a year to reaffirm its virtues and intentions, or they couldn't participate in the family bank.

Subsequently, the Rothschilds' wealth compounded and grew as it passed to future generations."[11]

Mayer Rothschild used his wealth as an opportunity to instill the family with values, grow their collective knowledge and affirm their sense of unity and purpose. He prepared his family to receive, and they were receiving wealth of a different kind.

As I said before, I'm a Proverbs reader, and one verse that has stuck with me is, Proverbs 13:22—"A good man leaves an inheritance to his children's children."

Structuring a Legacy

So, how does a person do that? How do we effect not just our children, but our children's children, or our children's children's children? Personally, I plan to see my great-grandchildren, and even my great-greats. How do I pass on the things I know, and is my legacy to just my children, or my family? Or is it my friends, my greater community?

Let's take a second to look at the various ways we can leave our legacy, and perhaps ways to be more Rothschild, less Vanderbilt.

---

[11] Douglas Andrew. Warner Business Books. 2005. "Missed Fortune 101." 11-13.

Wills

When we think of legacy planning, a lot of people go automatically to wills. This is the fundamental document we associate with legal estate planning. A will is where we state who gets what. Wills can be as broad-brush as the "sell it all and divide the proceeds according to X children" approach, or as detailed as listing who will inherit each prized family heirloom. Yet, these are considered the "basics" for a reason. Wills can transfer ownership, but there are many things they can't do, such as:

- Avoid probate
- Avoid taxation on properties
- Override the terms of beneficiary designations on financial contracts
- Dictate the "terms" of possession—such as who should get X asset if Person A dies
- Help mitigate sticky issues of survivorship in the case of a blended family

Wills are certainly the starting point for legacy planning, but they are not the final word, in large part because of probate.

Probate

Probate is the legal process of determining a will's validity. During the probate process, anyone can petition the court to read the contents of the will (and I mean *anyone*), so a family's assets become a matter of open record. Additionally, during probate anyone can throw their hat into the ring, asking the judge to consider if the deceased accidentally left them out of the will. Even those of us who aren't dedicated tabloid readers would have to be completely oblivious to have not heard the plights of families such as Anna Nicole Smith's or Michael Jackson's. Their fortunes and family dirty laundry was publicly aired to the point we all wished they would cover it up. Meanwhile, their estates were eaten away in legal fees. During the probate process, the estate is tied up, as well, meaning caregivers may not have access to funding to cover even basic expenses for children of the deceased. And probate can be long. In the aforementioned Anna Nicole Smith case, the probate case lasted for 20 years and raged across multiple states.

Trusts

So, how do we avoid probate and accomplish those other line items that wills can't? You probably are at least nominally familiar with trusts. They hold assets and make one person, the trustee, the owner of the property, often acting as the fiduciary (someone who is required to act in the best interest) for another person or people. This is a basic definition, because trusts can be revocable or irrevocable, they can have special parameters or limitations, and seem to be as big or small as we make them. They can:

- Avoid probate
- Avoid types of taxation
- Be named as the beneficiary of financial contracts
- Dictate how and when beneficiaries will receive payments
- Mitigate rights of survivorship and transference in tricky situations for blended families

Now, I'd like to be clear: The beneficiary line of financial contracts trumps wills and trusts. For you to be sure your property is in the trust, you will need to designate the trust as the beneficiary for that financial vehicle.

Part of what makes trusts so advantageous for blended families is the ability to control survivorship. For instance, in situations like the couple I mentioned in the last chapter, instead of taking the risk that his wife would have to move in the case of his death, the husband could have titled their home to a trust. He could dictate the terms of the trust so that it would pass first to his wife and then to his children from a previous marriage after her death. Then, everyone wins. The man's children would get their inheritance, but his wife wouldn't be turned out in the cold while grieving the loss of her husband.

My final word on wills and trusts is that all of this sort of estate planning should be done in conjunction with a competent attorney who specializes in this area. At CFG, I have formed special relationships with local estate planning attorneys so that we can cross-coordinate and strive to be as tax-efficient as possible.

What Will You Pass On?

One thing that I've learned over the years and from working with people of different backgrounds and values is there are different types of wealth. There are social assets (what we pay taxes for and the charities and community organizations we donate to), financial assets (401(k)s, stocks, life insurance, real estate, etc.) and knowledge assets (such as the values I've passed on to my sons, or the techniques and strategies I've worked on in my business...you might say this book is a knowledge asset!).

Our mission statement at CFG is "Building Wealth That Lasts." We want to help people build, enjoy and pass their wealth on, but does all of that matter much if it's here today and gone tomorrow? If we've saved and built wealth, do we want to lose it with bad decisions? We also may want to pass it on to our children, but there is also an eternal component. To me, this makes legacy planning that much more critical, because once you have departed this earth, there aren't any do-overs.

The name "Nicholas Winton" may not mean much to you at a glance. Winton became unexpectedly involved in World War II when, while planning a ski trip, he was sidetracked through a letter correspondence with a friend into Czechoslovakia. During his odd sidebar journey, Winton started a "host family" system that diverted Jewish children from trains bound for Auschwitz with their parents. Through forgeries, falsified documents and copious bribes, Winton was able to save a verified 669 children, and possibly more.

For years, his heroism was forgotten with a scrapbook of letters, correspondence and forged documents in an attic. It wasn't until 1988—five decades later—that his wife discovered his deeds. He shrugged it off, saying the scrapbook was worthless and could easily be discarded. Many of us have seen the perennially viral video, though, from the BBC program, "That's Life." A few of the rescued children—children no longer—step forward to shake Winton's hand. As the man dabs his eyes, he is told the entire audience is made of those he rescued and their own children. [12]

Winton died in 2015 at age 106, after receiving a knighthood and earning the reputation of being "the British Oskar Schindler." What if he had passed on and his family never knew what he had done? On the one hand, his silence speaks volumes of his personal humility. On the other hand, if you were his child, wouldn't you want to know this about your parent?

I think we can all agree this is a remarkable legacy to pass on. When it comes to the end of your own life, what would you say if you could speak at your own funeral, and what would others say about you?

This is very much the stuff that will determine how we structure our assets, and the way we use our time and relationships. And hopefully, at the end of it all, we will have the chance to hear, "Well done, good and faithful servant, enter into the joy of your Master."

---

[12] Daniel Victor. New York Times. July 1, 2015. "Nicholas Winton's 'Most Emotional Moment.'" https://www.nytimes.com/2015/07/01/world/europe/nicholas-wintons-most-emotional-moment.html?action=click&contentCollection=Europe&module=RelatedCoverage&region=EndOfArticle&pgtype=article.

CHAPTER EIGHT

Does Your Plan Have Integrity?

Y ou know your values. You have your cashflow under control. You have an investment strategy that supports a strong income source. You're smart about taxes. You built protection into the plan, and your legacy is a work in progress. Now you just have to make sure it's all working together.

You might think it easy, but that's where a lot of people's plans fall apart. Part of this is what I like to call cleaning out the financial junk drawer. We all tend to make financial decisions in the rush of life, making each one at a time as life comes at us. Even when we jump out of the rat race, life doesn't come to a total standstill. My clients tend to find their social calendar fill up every bit as fast as their work calendar. That's why it's so important to model and "game" our plan, to make sure that it all makes sense individually, but that it also makes sense as a whole.

Financial Blueprints

The best analogy I can give you for building a strong financial and retirement plan is the process of building a home. I am very familiar with the building process, having grown up in the building trades with my father and older brother. My hands were involved from the foundation to the framing and mechanicals all the way to the finished product. I have also designed and acted as my own general contractor for numerous offices and homes over the years. I'd like to tie that insight into this chapter with the idea of blueprints. A set of blueprints will include a site plan, the foundation plan, and views of the exterior—the front, back, and sides of your home. You'll have a page for the framing and mechanics of your heating and cooling, you'll have a page for plumbing, a page of fixtures and electrical specifications, a page for the hardware, doors and cabinetry. When you don't have these drawings all assembled together, there is ALWAYS miscommunication.

You may also remember my offices have just moved into a new space, one that was built well before I entered the scene. While I've done the best to remodel the building and get it up to specs, the process was a heavy reinforcement for how much easier the job can be when you are working from complete blueprints. If all the elements of a home aren't working together or were built incorrectly, things may be missing. I'm sure I'm not the only one who's marveled at a new construction project only to hear weeks later that it burned down or collapsed. Or maybe it's not as dramatic as all that—maybe it's just that the doors don't close all the way, or things that drop on the floor roll a certain direction.

Am I on bedrock? Am I above the floodplain? How efficient is my home? Will I pay out the wazoo for utilities? These are all questions that translate into retirement as much as they do in home building.

I built my business on Proverbs 24:3-4. In it, Solomon says, "By wisdom a house is built, by understanding it is established, by knowledge its rooms are filled with pleasant and precious riches."

Do you think Solomon was talking about a house? No. Neither do I. There are many applications for us. In working with my clients, I want them to be as knowledgeable as they want to be about finance and retirement, to understand how money should work in a coordinated and integrated process and to make wise decisions about their retirement so the rooms in their lives are filled with pleasant and precious riches.

Surprises

One thing I've noticed when it comes to both building and retirement planning is that surprises are rarely beneficial. Seldom does a contractor call late at night to say, "Hey, everything's coming together way ahead of schedule, and under budget, too!"

This is why we should have someone else go through our financial houses and look at every component—each layer, each room— once it's put together to see where errors or omissions occurred and identify them with us. How often do things show up in your own home that you wish you would have known about earlier? Or, alternately, how often do we see little things we think we'll get to later, and then when later comes, we regret not fixing them immediately? Like when a spot in the ceiling turns out to mean your plumbing is leaking, or a small crack in the wall turns out to be foundation problems?

Through your working years, others preached about how to put money into your plans like a 401(k), 457, 403(b) or IRA, but did anyone show you strategies for how to come back out of those plans? What's your strategy for minimizing the taxes when you come out of those plans or when you begin to distribute that money? What about your investments? Are you minimizing the risk of your portfolio? Are you minimizing the taxes on your portfolio, minimizing the fees? Is your money MOVING or is it staying in one place? Is it moving so it can multiply and increase benefits, or is it locked up? The real way to find out if there are leaky pipes in your financial plan is to build a model to simulate and test it. You should know how your current strategies will work in the future, and whether your plan will work. A PLAN THAT CAN'T ADAPT TO WORK IN ALL CIRCUMSTANCES IS NO PLAN AT ALL.

We have modeling software at CFG, which we use to stress test and "what-if" current and new strategies. I like to think of it similar to chess—master chess players look several moves ahead to see what the most effective move of a piece on the board will be. If you took away the structure, the rules, the looking ahead and the gameboard, what would you have? Just a bunch of random pieces. That's how many people's financial plans look when they first come in. They're a little haphazard, but once we organize their financial pieces and begin to process, we can start to get a feel for how their financial assets, insurances, wills and trusts will all act together under different circumstances, how one might affect another, and where we have the potential for unwanted surprises. Once we know where those gaps are in our plan, we can work through the process to repair them.

I have a client who kept a portion of his retirement assets with our office while he was working. He had the rest of his assets with another investment firm. As with every client, we would evaluate the way all of his assets might work together. We simulated where he would pull income from and how his portfolio might react to different circumstances. When we had recommendations for him, we would walk him through why we thought he should go one way instead of another, discussing his financial model and personal goals. The other office contacted him once a year to see if he wanted to make any change in his investments. This gentleman was an engineer by trade, and as he approached retirement, he looked at his situation and started to evaluate which office he would use as his advisor in retirement.

He decided to move his assets over to our office, in large part because of the comprehensive approach we take in examining not only his investments, but also how he was going to generate income he could depend on, to think ahead and look to minimize taxes, how he was going to protect his assets from confiscation, how much liquidity he should have, were his estate plans set up properly. He said that, while he knew "the movie won't play out exactly that way," it gave him greater confidence in how he was positioned to take the surprises out of his retirement. His retirement was now on a solid foundation.

Integrity

The real purpose of this chapter is for you to ask yourself if your total retirement planning process has integrity. Among the books I enjoy is Henry Cloud's "Integrity." It is full of definitions of wonderful words, among them "character," which he defines as, "The ability to meet the demands of reality." His fascinating understanding of integrity clearly took root in my own understanding. From French and Latin roots, integrity finds relatives in words like intact, integral and entirety. To loosely quote the book, if something has integrity, it means it works well, is undivided, integrated, intact and uncorrupted. This concept I think applies just as much to one's financial and retirement plan as it does to any other area of our lives. So, I have borrowed this thought from Dr. Cloud and applied it to a retirement plan.

"The whole thing is working well, it is undivided, integrated, intact and uncorrupted. All the different parts are working together and delivering the functions they are designed to deliver. It's running on all cylinders."

You may call it a holistic approach to retirement—taking a look at the totality of the picture instead of limiting our gaze to any single part. That's part of what Your RetireWise Path is all about. For example, you can only be truly tax efficient if you are considering taxes for your income sources, investments, Social Security, and considering how your assets will be passed on when you are gone, still in a tax-efficient manner.

This is one of the reasons that I purchased and renovated the former Friends University satellite campus building in Topeka, Kansas, which is where we are located. I want my workspace to reflect this holistic view, by allowing people to have a sort of one-stop-shop for retirement. We have a tax professional and an estate planning attorney in the building with me, and perhaps we'll even find room for the "retirement therapist" that one couple told me I should have! This coordinated effort with other professionals gives our clients confidence in their retirement path.

A plan's integrity is more important than ever when we reach retirement, because at retirement, we've likely accumulated most of the assets we're going to have for retirement. Unless you have lots of passive income sources, retirement severs your main income stream, which is "You at Work." Yet, once those random assets become the main source of your income, reality quickly sets in. My son wrote the chapter on investing, and he spoke of his love of mountains. We don't have a lot of mountains or high elevation in Kansas, but from my experiences in states like our neighbor Colorado, it's fair to say that the strategies and techniques you use to ascend a mountain are different than the ones you should use to come down. That's where we at CFG really shine—coming down the mountain. We all want to get down the mountain successfully, meaning we want:

- Finances that produce long-term wealth
- Substantial retirement income
- Minimized taxes
- Reduced risk and cost
- Well-preserved legacy
- Financial plans that are organized, flexible and easy to manage and control

You can't have all of those things, really, if all the parts of your plan are working separately and uncoordinated. You want to have everything working for one purpose, all in one direction.

Recently a 74-year-old came into my office with a large stock portfolio. He had been managing it himself, and had clearly done well. I asked him, "Why did you feel like you needed someone else?" He said, "We could earn 0 percent and we'd be fine, but it's not easy to manage anymore."

He understood that, with so many assets and so many moving parts, it was time to have help. His portfolio had grown to the point he couldn't continue to evaluate it for tax efficiency, cost-effectiveness and adequate diversity and protection anymore by himself. He was concerned for his wife and wanted to work with someone his wife felt comfortable with and could count on if he were to pass on before her.

I admired his humility—too often I see people who are taking a reactive approach to their finances when there is an economic change or because of world events, instead of people such as that gentleman who are proactive and purposeful about their financial choices. Having an integrated process helps us take the emotions out of our financial decisions, and can help us stay on firm foundations.

The title of this book is "Exiting the Rat Race." Life can be that, a rat race filled with uncertainty and not having a clear purpose in the decisions being made based on your values.

So, I have to ask you, does your plan have integrity?

CHAPTER NINE

Finding an Advisor

O ver the years I have people contact us who have never heard of me, never met me, but were invited and attended one of our seminars/workshops and decided to come to our office and visit with me. We always ask why they chose to come in and visit and share their concerns. Recently, one gentleman told me that he'd seen the designations behind my name, RICP, ChFC, CLU, and thought I might know something. Admittedly, I am well educated and have a lot of experience in the area of personal finance and economics, but it is also humbling, for I feel I have to prove myself even more, in part because, in my experience, designations are not the only criteria on which to evaluate a financial professional. That's not to say they aren't important, just that they aren't the *only* important quality.

Make no mistake—who helps you through the financial process in retirement can make a big difference. During your working years, you likely had a financial professional who managed the company account for your 401(k) plan, pension or similar. Perhaps you even had an outside person who managed some of your private funds. Maybe your car and house insurance agent also sold you a life insurance policy, and you likely had someone who did your taxes every spring. But, were all of those professionals working together, in the same direction, proactively? Probably not.

You need to give serious consideration to whoever it is who will guide you to and through retirement. This is not like any other point in your financial life—your financial advisor will be responsible for being honest with you and guiding you with your best interest in mind. They will be instrumental in setting you up for what will hopefully be financial success for the rest of your life. I don't want to be alarming or dramatic, but I also want to impart the importance of your decision in whom to place your trust.

To help you make this decision, following are some criteria on which a good advisor may be evaluated. These are the qualities that I believe are universal to a good advisor. Whether you are in Topeka, Kansas; Seattle, Washington; Sarasota, Florida; or Timbuktu, I think these characteristics are essential.

Licensing

If you're considering a financial professional, you are going to want to evaluate what services he or she is licensed to provide. In my chapter on income, I touched on the "this versus that" mentality of some professionals who are only licensed to provide one area of service. You will want to be sure that the office you are working with has the ability to give advice and guidance about multiple products, from insurance to securities.

Some questions to ask when you're evaluating a potential advisor:

- What licenses do they possess?
- Has a state or federal regulatory body fined them or imposed restrictions on their business for any reason?
- Do they have open legal complaints against them?

Education

You don't need to have a college degree to hang up a shingle as a financial professional. This may or may not be important to you—as with many fields, someone with years of experience and no degree can be a much better asset to you than someone fresh out of college.

When I say education, I mean much more than a degree. I also mean designations. You know, the ones that sound like the Aretha Franklin song, "R-E-S-P-E-C-T." I have several designations, and they all stand for something (and no, RICP doesn't stand for Rest In © Peace). The Retirement Income Certified Professional, Chartered Financial Consultant and Chartered Life Underwriter designations I earned from The American College of Financial Services. I stay current on them all through hours of continued education every year. Another designation that has a strong degree of credibility is the Certified Financial Planner designation.

Not all designations are created equal, however. While many certificates and designations require hours of ongoing education and proof of successful planning processes, others are little more than a fee and registration on a website. That's why this criterion needs careful consideration—it can be a strong indicator of an advisor's commitment to ongoing education, and testify to their willingness to keep up with current trends and practices. Alternately, it can speak to a financial professional's decision to choose flashy designations over the ones that take hard work.

Questions to ask in this category:
- Do you have any additional designations or certifications?
- What organization did you earn them from?
- What sort of coursework/experience did they require?
- What kind of continued education do you engage in?
- How do you stay up-to-date with market trends and strategies?

Experience

To return to the mountain analogy, the same tools and strategies that took you up the mountain will not necessarily be the same ones that get you down. The way you saved and invested in your youth will not be much assistance when it comes to figuring out how to withdraw those monies in a tax-advantageous and legacy-minded way when it comes time to get income in retirement. Is it your goal to get up the mountain? Or do you want to get down the mountain safely?

The question of experience is also important because this industry has such a high rate of burnout. It's hard to get solid numbers on burnout, but in 2016, there were about 36,000 "trainee" advisors, while more than 29,500 advisors washed out of the profession with less than five years of experience.[13] Someone who only has a few years under their belt may not be in business tomorrow, but someone who has stuck it out for a decade is more likely to be around for the long haul. So, check to be sure the head of whatever office you're working with has a good deal of experience. You don't want to have to change advisors just a few years into retirement.

In my office, we focus mainly on getting down the mountain. It's what we do all day, every day; helping people develop individual strategies and approaches for withdrawing their assets in an efficient way, with all elements of their plan working in alignment with their values. And I have three decades of experience doing it!

Here, the questions you might be ready to ask are:

- How long have you been in this profession?
- How long have you been with this particular office or group?
- What does your "typical" client look like?

---

[13] Alessandra Malito. InvestmentNews. May 29, 2016. "The time is now for young financial advisers." http://www.investmentnews.com/article/20160529/FREE/160529937/the-time-is-now-for-young-financial-advisers.

- Do you have a specialty?
- How much experience do you have working with the distribution and preservation phase of financial life?
- What portion of your clients do you help transition into retirement?
- What are your business continuation plans if and when you are no longer in the picture?

Holistic/Integrated Approach

This ties back into the idea of licensing, but is slightly different. Basically, is your advisor not only licensed to provide different services, but also capable of operating similar to a quarterback in working with a network of cross-professionals such as estate planning, tax, legal, etc.?

Is your advisor capable of positioning you in retirement for multiple sources of income, or are they singular in nature—are they pulling your income from a single source? They SHOULD develop strategies with many sources of income.

You want to be sure that you're working with a macro-thinker. Are they a micro-advisor, or a MACRO-advisor? Micro-advisors have laser focus, but aren't thinking about events beyond the two or three in front of them. A macro-advisor can take a broad view, zeroing in on trouble-spots, but also seeing where everything fits in a broader context.

Is your advisor calling shots based on a big-picture view, or do they have tunnel vision, focused on only one or two specific issues? Think of how your results might be different if all of your professionals communicate, versus what it might look like if they don't. In this case, the financial advisor should be able to coordinate the work of other professionals—think of them as the general contractor. Not only should he or she do a specific trade competently, they should also evaluate the efforts of others to be sure each one is doing their job for you. The contractor may not do plumbing or wiring, but they should be able to see if they plumber isn't doing the job right and help you take corrective action.

So, a few questions to ask your advisor in this arena:

- Do you consider yourself comprehensive?
- Do you have a working knowledge of taxation and general efficiency?
- How do you help your clients protect their assets and prepare for health care in retirement?
- What is your investment philosophy?
- Do you help your clients with things like debt management and cashflow?
- Do you have strategic partnerships with other professionals, such as tax planners or attorneys?

Continuation in Mind with Adequate Support

Continuity is important when it comes to financial strategies. If you bounced to a new advisor every few years, it would be hard to have stability in your planning and process, right? That's why you should look for a professional who is legacy-minded and has an adequate support staff. For one thing, you should know what your advisor's succession plan is. When will he or she retire, and to whom will their clients go? If your financial professional had the misfortune of being hit by a bus tomorrow, what would you do and where would you go?

Right now, some financial advisors operate as mavericks. They are understaffed and lack the fundamentals of a succession plan. Listen, I get the urge to be independent. That's what my office is. But a competent advisor should at least have a plan for the what-ifs. In the case where an advisor doesn't have a succession plan, his or her book of business (meaning, their registry of clients) is sold off to the highest bidder. That sure isn't what I'd want to happen for me mid-retirement.

In my office, I have a long-term succession plan. While I hope to stay active in my business for a long, long time, and while I have no immediate plans to retire, this is part of why I have brought on my son, Jon, along with other advisors. He is a big part of my legacy plan. He has established relationships with all of our current clients, and will gradually assume ownership of the business so if I'm ever ready to retire or if I–God forbid—depart this world earlier than I intend, no one will have to move their assets or be thrown for a loop.

Another part of the continuity is the office staff. Is the financial advisor you're considering readily available to answer your calls? If he or she isn't, do they have enough competent staff members who are? There's no exact right number of staff people that meet some certain criteria, this is more of a gut thing. The bottom line is whether you get to talk to a real person in a timely manner when you need them and whether the firm functions as an ongoing entity.

To understand whether these basic elements of office balance are in alignment, ask your advisor:

- What is your succession plan?
- Who would help me with retirement if something happened to you?
- When do you plan to retire?
- How many office support staff do you have?
- If I call and no one answers, how long will it be before I receive a response from your office?

Individual-Focused

A financial advisor worth their salt will focus on your individual needs, and must be a good fit for you, personally. When you find the right fit for an advisor who will help guide you to and through retirement, it can be a decades-long relationship, so you need to be sure you're working with someone who you will feel comfortable with for the long haul.

The right advisor will listen carefully to you, your story and your desires. They will ask lots of questions and spend more time trying to understand your values and goals than they do *telling* you answers. They will be sure you understand what's going on with your money, explaining techniques in real terms and not just using fancy technical jargon. An advisor should be accessible and show they are concerned about you personally. How can they help you plan for your dreams and goals if they don't know or care what those goals are?

Although I have some clients from similar backgrounds, their financial lives still often look dissimilar, because they have different values, goals and dreams. That's what you should be looking for. If you feel like you walk into an office and are immediately pegged as a certain "bracket" of client, or like you've been given the "Option A, B or C" treatment, feel free to walk back out. After all, isn't it time to exit the rat race?

A last point about an advisor's individualistic approach centers on what we might call bedside manner. Basically, are they respectful of other people? You might think that this would go without saying, but you'd be wrong. Often this is clearer with spouses—some advisors have a tendency to speak solely to one of the partners, typically the husband. This is just plain arrogance. I've had many widows come into my office, tired of being talked down to by a previous financial advisor. Any good professional will be listening and speaking to both members, period.

So, this isn't a checklist of questions for the advisor so much as it is a checklist of questions to ask yourself after a conversation with someone you are considering:

- Did you personally get along with this person?
- Did they seem genuinely concerned and caring?
- Who did most of the talking during the conversation?
- Did they answer your questions with everyday terminology, or did their answers leave you more confused?
- If you're married, did both of you feel addressed, or did one of you feel left out of the conversation?
- Did the advisor make you feel uncomfortable or belittled at any point?

Objective

The last but not least quality of a good financial professional is about their objectivity. Can they be depended on to give you the best recommendation they can, regardless of other factors? As I like to say, dependability is the best ability.

This sense of objectivity goes by another name in legal and financial circles. It's called the "fiduciary" standard. A fiduciary is someone who is legally bound to act in the best interests of another person. For instance, the executor of a will must do what was in the best interests (and express directive) of the deceased. A medical fiduciary is someone who acts in the best interests of someone who can't make their own medical decisions. In finance, it means that a financial advisor is acting in the best interest of the client. As an Investment Adviser Representative who has passed a Series 65 securities exam, I am a fiduciary. Some people mistakenly think all financial professionals are held to this standard, but that is incorrect. Most financial professionals must follow a "suitability" standard. That means they recommend products that are in line with a person's goals and are affordable. A fiduciary must go further than that, though. Instead of merely recommending products that are suitable, a fiduciary must do what is in the best interest of the client without regard to commissions, fees or incentives.

So, in addition to disregarding commissions, fees and incentives, I think an integral part of objectivity is the independence to recommend a variety of products, regardless of what brands or companies sell them. For instance, a professional at Big Box Brokerage might only be able to shop around with Big Box Product A or Big Box Product B. I think it's important for your financial advisor to use products from many different companies, so they have a broader range to pick from to find the best product to fit your needs.

So, in this category, there are only two questions you have to ask:

- Are you independent?
- Are you a fiduciary?

In my 31 years of experience in this industry, I have seen firsthand how smoothly retirement planning can go when all of the gears are greased, all the cogs are connecting, and all of these qualifications are in place. Like a well-built machine, the client-advisor relationship steadily churns through the questions, the what-ifs, and the uncertainties. Alternately, when these things aren't in place, I see clients forced to change gears mid-retirement. It disappoints me to see other professionals act recklessly toward people who are in or who are entering what can be a vulnerable stage of life.

The first clients who I helped retire were my father and my father-in-law. I was proud and nervous when they asked me to handle their retirements. While I'm sure that both of these men, whom I admired, thought of it as a way to help ensure my future success, they also knew I would not let them down. I remember being wide-eyed at how much influence I would have on *their* futures. It's a responsibility I resolved to never take lightly.

Personally, I believe that everyone deserves a financial advisor who can meet them where they're at, both literally and metaphorically. I say literally, because I have one widowed client, she lives a little out of the way, but I know that if I didn't physically visit her in her home, she would likely never come in to follow up on her financial goals and situation. Because her input is paramount to maintaining an integrated and individual-focused plan, I make it a point to visit her in her home at times.

At CFG, we hold fast to our vision of "Financial Wisdom for Every Client"—if I can't identify with where a client is at, how can I help them make wise decisions? Or mission is, "Building Wealth That Lasts." My son, Jon, is instrumental in this vision. Part of building something lasting is having the infrastructure in place that will continue to support growth and services. Jon is instrumental in this legacy—my clients know we take our relationships seriously, and that our offices will be here to support them, their visions and dreams, even when someday I am not.

Just as your personal values are the underlying factor of your whole retirement plan, our values underscore every area of our practice. I encourage you, even after all of your other questions have been answered, to consider if your values and the values of your intended advisor are aligned—especially for retirement, you want to be moving in the same direction.

CHAPTER TEN

Generosity

"We make a living by what we get, we make a life by what we give."
– Winston Churchill

Before we reach the conclusion, I'd like to take a moment to address one area that is incredibly important to me: generosity. You may be wondering, why are we addressing it here? Isn't that part of income and legacy and all that? And you'd be right. But I think it deserves its own section because, in my personal observations, some people slow down their generosity and giving in retirement because of uncertainty. When they are uncertain about their own financial situations, they don't give to the organizations that help those in precarious situations. If we build certainty into our financial lives, we are more confident to be generous while supporting the lifestyles we desire and have become accustomed to.

I believe most people in their hearts want to be generous, so, like with building certainty into the plan, we must begin with the end in mind. Make giving a part of your strategy from the outset, and then you won't question it later. After all, if a financial strategy is really just a means of supporting your values, and one of your values is generosity, then your financial strategy should allow you the room to be generous. I think more people would remain generous in later life if they just knew how.

Personally, I have several worthy organizations that are close to my heart. Young Life, a Christian ministry that comes alongside kids and college students, shows them the love of Jesus and introduces them to Him, is among them. My wife and I were involved early in the Topeka area Young Life. One of the biggest events for the group every year is summer camp. When kids go to summer camp, they are told it will be the best week of their life, and I've never met a kid who came away from camp disagreeing! My son, Andy, is the area director of the thriving and vibrant Topeka Young Life. What a joy it is for my wife and I to serve this ministry we believe in alongside our son and daughter-in-law, Angelyn.

Several years into the ministry, Young Life was introduced at Topeka High, an inner city high school. To help establish the Young Life vision at T-High, we needed to take kids to summer camp, which meant a long ride to Frontier Ranch in Buena Vista, Colorado. We took 13 boys, many of whom had never been out of state, and some of whom had never even been outside of Topeka.

The bus ride there smelled of surly teen machismo. The kids who got on the bus were all very guarded. They had no idea what they were headed into. Even the experience of getting off the bus was disorienting for them—per Young Life camp tradition, there was a crowd of people whooping, hollering and blasting music while the kids exited. I can still remember the confusion. Down to the biggest, toughest-looking kid, the boys' eyes were wide, and they couldn't help at least half-smiling nervously.

That was only the beginning. Through the rest of the week, they learned to recognize their machoism as a defense mechanism, and started to learn how to drop it. They started to form relationships with each other and the others at camp, treat others with respect, and build a solid faith foundation. Many of these kids came from unstable homes, where parents were absent, either literally or practically. Through this experience, they all changed in a big way. They made a pact to go back and change their high school—and they did.

I share this story because it's easy to be generous with your family, but there are more opportunities and often a greater need to be generous in your community, country and around the globe, even if it isn't always as easy. Historically, some of the best armies were those in which the front lines' shields were doubly strong, made to cover a single man as well as the man standing next to him. With this overlapping protection, the front line could advance well into enemy territory with few or zero casualties. Often, our communities need these overlapping shields.

At least some of this community-mindedness has scriptural inspiration for me. Proverbs 11:24-25 "There is one who scatters yet increases more and there is one who withholds more than is right but it leads to poverty. The generous will be made wealthy, the waterer will be watered himself and be made whole."

A lot of times we hold onto things out of fear, but sometimes we see people give and receive in turn. We hear all the time that it is better to give than to receive, there's more joy in giving, etc., it's just hard to live that out sometimes. If generosity is a VALUE on which you have built your retirement, though, then you will likely find yourself still able to carry that out.

There's another gem about this in Proverbs 3, "Honor the lord with all your possessions and with the first fruits of all your increase so your barns will be filled with plenty and your vats will overflow with new wine."

You don't give *in order to receive*, that's not the reason, but in giving we receive. At CFG, we want to be generous with what we know, we give it freely. We've always felt by giving of our knowledge, we tend to gain even more. The only way to prosper in financial knowledge of course, is by putting it into practice, not by being stingy about it!

I have a client who was getting ready for retirement. He was a giver, both in terms of his time and his money. In his own right, he was wealthy, and part of his retirement plan was to be sure that even in retirement he could continue giving at the same level to his church and other organizations of worthy causes. He recognized the support he gave was important, and so his retirement plan asked the question of "Can I still give at the level I currently do?" We built his plan around his lifestyle—including and especially his giving—and found unique ways of fulfilling those desires.

I believe most people would LIKE to be remembered as generous, similar to the way this man surely will be. They just don't know how. Yet, as his example shows, it is more likely that you will be able to achieve being generous if it is a built-in part of your lifestyle, as habitual as paying the bills.

There are numerous strategies you can use to make sure your charitable giving is tax efficient, and which can help you balance your own need for income sources with your desire to give selflessly. One strategy is a charitable remainder trust, or CRT. Although it seems to be an underused strategy, CRTs have been around since the Tax Reform Act of 1969. The act was mostly concerned with the creation of the alternative minimum tax that I discussed in the tax chapter, but it also changed a few of the conditions surrounding the charitable capabilities of assets such as an irrevocable trust.

A CRT can be an especially tax-efficient strategy if someone has a highly appreciated asset like an IRA, stocks or real estate. When someone puts an asset in a CRT, they can then sell the asset at its full value without paying taxes on the appreciation. They can even withdraw a certain amount of the assets for income, and the IRS will calculate what will remain in the trust (remember the "remainder" is the R part of a CRT) when the period for income distributions is ended. Based off of the calculated remainder, you can then take a tax deduction, which can be particularly helpful in a year you might need to offset any other large tax burdens.

Here is an illustration. Let's say a 65-year-old has $750,000 in a stock that has a basis of $250,000. They could sell the stock and give the proceeds after tax to some worthy place. But what if they first gave the $750,000 in stock to a CRT, then it was sold with no tax? Here is what happens.

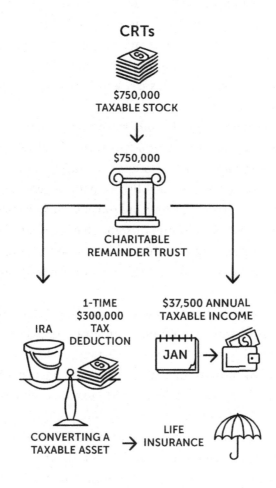

The CRT holds the $750,000 for the charity. The donor is able to take a deduction for the remainder of the $750,000 after taking income over their life expectancy. The income will be calculated at about 5 percent of the $750,000, or $37,500 of income, which is all taxable. The tax deduction will be about $300,000. What can they do with the $300,000 tax deduction? What if they had a $300,000 IRA? This IRA could then be converted to a Roth IRA using the tax deduction. The donor now has income from the CRT, which is taxable and can take income from the Roth IRA, tax-free. The extra income can be used to purchase life insurance to replace the asset given to the charity if the donor wishes to give this to their family and not disinherit anyone. This is a win for everyone: the charity, the donor and the family.

You can let the tax people and attorneys figure out the complicated part; the important piece of this is that it allows you to give yourself some income while also ensuring anything left over goes to charity and allows you to establish a legacy of generosity.

We all want to have meaning and purpose in retirement, and in our lives on the whole. To me, this goes hand in hand with being generous and supporting our communities. Maintaining generosity means planning ahead, building this into our lifestyle and income ahead of time.

If your plan is well-integrated, it can make charitable giving more feasible—if you have enough put away for emergencies, for income, maybe if you've put away a certain fund for a gift to your children... All of those things can be taken together, made tax-efficient, and used to create a legacy that extends far beyond your bloodline.

It makes me think a little of Cornelius Vanderbilt, from the chapter about legacy. As noted there, he wasn't known for his generosity—certainly not to the extent of someone like his contemporary, Andrew Carnegie, whose name graces numerous libraries.

Yet, in a twist of fate, one of his longest-lasting legacies is Vanderbilt University, the sole institute to which he donated a notable sum. The hundreds of millions of dollars he left to his family is notable now only as one of several remarkable stories of squandered fortunes. This isn't perhaps the best reason to be generous and charitable, but it is certainly food for thought.

I look at taking care of the needy as being essential for a life well-lived. Jesus tells us that true religion is taking care of widows and orphans, and in Topeka, it's easy to see this need. Thankfully, it's also to see those who are working to meet that need. We have one of the best shelters in the nation in the Topeka Rescue Mission. The local Harvesters feeds thousands every year. Young Life helps teens find a firm foundation in their otherwise ever-changing lives. These are some of the organizations that are doing the most good, and without them, our communities would be broken. But without generous people like you and me, these organizations wouldn't exist.

Whether you build charity into your income, or whether you intend to leave a sizeable asset like an endowment or trust to charity, the key is to think and plan ahead. Remember the words of the pastor I mentioned in the chapter on legacy, whose son had died prematurely? He said, "You are not ready to live until you are ready to die." There is truth in that statement.

Be Brilliant at the Basics

"The secret of getting ahead is getting started. The secret to getting started is breaking your complex overwhelming tasks into small, manageable tasks and then starting on the first one."
– Mark Twain

Thank you for sharing your time reading my thoughts. I'd like to leave you with a bit of wisdom I learned from the famed Samurai, Tom Cruise.

In "The Last Samurai," Cruise plays an American military captain involved in a military effort to westernize Japan. Sent to train a bunch of loyalist farmers, he and his untested trainees are soon overwhelmed by the rebel Samurai forces. The Samurai take Cruise's character captive, and soon begin to train him in their own fighting style.

Despite being a battle-tested fighter himself, Cruise looks downright clumsy as he begins training. Of course, as he progresses, his teachers aren't teaching him any new, exciting, mind-blowing moves. Instead, they are re-teaching the fundamentals of fighting. Of course, by the close, Cruise has learned the core of the Samurai code—"advanced techniques are the basics mastered."

This 17th century Samurai code is something we use as a touchstone in our office. Partly because we see it is often the fundamentals of someone's plan that puts it in jeopardy. Often, it's because someone is coming out of the accumulation stage of their life—they've been focused on growing their assets, somewhat awkwardly—and now they are trying to use the same techniques in preserving and taking distributions from those assets.

If advanced techniques are the basics mastered, what basics are you working from?

In the course of this book, I've outlined a sequence of what our team at CFG believes to be the basic sequence of how someone might approach retirement. It's the sequence of a well-thought-out, meaningful retirement. It's a process, really, not a product. I largely have avoided giving examples about how this process applies in specific situations because there truly is no one-size-fits all strategy. Even families with similar assets and lifestyles often leave my office with different strategies and plans. No matter how similar these families may look on the outside, they often have dissimilar goals and dreams. But by following the same process, they will still arrive at a well-thought-out, meaningful retirement.

If advanced techniques are the basics mastered, then one must be *brilliant* at the basics.

Mastering the Basics: Cashflow and Income

Remember, there's no retirement without income. There are a few key questions that can help you identify whether you have mastered this basic.

- Does your incoming cashflow exceed outgoing expenses?
- Are your assets positioned properly for income that will continue the lifestyle you want?

- How much of your income is stable, or better yet, guaranteed?
- Have you examined the options you have for taking your Social Security benefit?
- Are there multiple income sources you will have in retirement?

Mastering the Basics: Investing

When it comes to investing, remember: Once you are within a few years of retirement, you won't have time to make up for unfortunate investing decisions like you do when you're in your accumulation phase. While investing for growth is key to beating inflation over the years, you don't want to be in a position where you're depending on risk-based assets for a basic level of income.

- Do you know how much risk your investment portfolio carries?
- Are your investments in line with your comfort level?
- Are you properly positioned to potentially grow your assets over time?
- Are you diversified, both in terms of the companies in which you are invested and in terms of the financial products you're using?
- Will your basic income and lifestyle suffer in the event of a market downturn?

Mastering the Basics: Taxes and Efficiency

No one can predict the tax environment, but if you remember the discussion in the tax chapter about the national debt, I think you'll agree it's better to prepare for the worst and hope for the best. While inflation can erode your assets' value over time, taxes and fees can take a bite out of your assets in the very immediate here and now.

- Are you prepared for higher taxes?
- Are you properly positioned to take advantage of temporary tax reductions?
- Do you/your advisor work closely with a true tax *planner* to be proactive about tax efficiency?
- Do you know what you pay for fees and expenses in your investment portfolio?
- Do you have a strategy for withdrawing highly appreciated tax-deferred assets?

Mastering the Basics: Protection

Even if your investments and income are tax-efficient and properly structured, if you don't have an adequate amount of insurance or liquidity, you are exposing it all to some hefty risks.

- Do you have sufficient liquidity to meet any emergency?
- Do you have enough money set aside to take advantage of significant opportunities or to make a big purchase?
- If married, what if either of you has a premature death, resulting in a loss of income?
- How do you intend to fund your care if you or a loved one has a significant health event or a prolonged illness?
- Do you have enough insurance protection in the case of a catastrophic event, such as a natural disaster or lawsuit?

Mastering the Basics: Legacy

If you've done your due diligence when it comes to planning for your own retirement and income, why not go a step further to delegate your assets after death. Everyone leaves a legacy, even if they leave zero material possessions. What do you want your legacy to be?

- What do you want to give and communicate to those who are dear to you?
- How well-written and documented are your wishes?
- Do you have a formal estate plan, including a will and/or trust?
- Are the beneficiary lines and designations up-to-date on all of your policies and assets?
- Are you working with a competent estate planning attorney who has helped you "what-if" your plans in various scenarios to be sure your estate is passed on in the manner you intended?
- What are your values? Where is your heart?

These questions are not complicated. The answers, solutions, strategies are very basic. Most advisors are just simply not implementing them. Work instead with someone who is keyed into the basics, and avoid plans that seem overly complicated and that an advisor can't explain to your satisfaction. The basics, the fundamentals, like having a process and working toward a goal, are the most important part of retirement planning. If those fundamentals aren't where your advisor's emphasis is, then they are not focused on retirement.

In our office, we have thought through many of the questions retirees should be asking themselves and have diligently pursued providing answers. The integrated process by which we do so is about being brilliant at the basics and always referring back to the foundation of your retirement.

It's important to remember that all of this financial preparation is still only the means of your retirement, not their end. When you envision dropping out of the rat race, hopefully you're looking toward brilliant basics in other areas of your life, too—faith, health, relationships...

If you are a couple, have you spent time dreaming and thinking through your retirement together? Are you on the same page? Have you shared your aspirations and values with each other?

Our lives are broken roughly into thirds. Our youth is largely on our own, and then comes the middle stage of life, centered on working and raising families. The last third should be about you enjoying the fruits of your labor, hopefully together. Yet, after the workaday world of the second stage of life, it is not uncommon for both spouses to look up, near or in retirement, and feel that they are looking at someone who is nearly a stranger. Once children have moved out, the house can seem strangely quiet.

What do you want retirement to look like? We cannot predict our own mortality with any degree of accuracy—if we did, countless actuaries would be out of jobs—but, statistically, many of us will have 25 to 35 years in retirement. That is a long time to feel rudderless. So, where's your sense of purpose and connection?

Have you ever been on a walk in the park and seen a nonagenarian jogger? Or maybe a nonagenarian couple, powering through a fast walk together? Do you stop and wish that could be you? I find many people are envious of these vibrant older folks, but few of us stop and think through the practical way to become that person. Regular workouts, healthy diet, active social life, meaningful relationships, community involvement—this is part of what retirement is about. If you have multiple decades to live, how do you want to live them?

These are some of the kinds of questions you should be asking yourself. Take time to write out your values. Write out where you are and where you want to go. Share those thoughts with the other important people in your life—spouse, children, etc. Whether it's pie-in-the-sky stuff or concrete points on a map, retirement can be an exhilarating adventure, and an excellent opportunity to deepen your relationships with those around you.

Thank you for taking the time to read this book. I hope you will take away some thoughts that serve you well on your retirement path. Remember, it's impossible to plan the next 25 to 30 years, financially or otherwise. Yet, with adherence to a process, brilliance at the basics, and careful attention to your values and goals, a trusted advisor can help you find the purpose you need to exit the rat race and not enter another one.

About Jeffry A. Vogel

Jeff Vogel, founder and president of CFG, Inc., found his calling to be a financial advisor in 1986. He was 29 years old and working in advertising. Jeff was very successful in his work, but was never truly attached to it, feeling a lack of purpose. Some of Jeff's customers were financial advisors and Jeff became deeply invested in understanding their approach in helping others. One of those advisors asked Jeff to join his practice; he never looked back.

Jeff received his Bachelor of Science degree in business administration from Fort Hays State University. His has earned his designations of Chartered Financial Consultant (ChFC), Chartered Life Underwriter (CLU) and Retirement Income Certified Professional (RICP), which uniquely qualify him to help his clients with retirement. Jeff is an Investment Adviser Representative and holds an insurance license in the state of Kansas. He is also a member of the National Association of Insurance and Financial Advisors (NAIFA) and the Society of Financial Services Professionals (SFP).

Jeff's values are rooted in his faith, his family and freedom. Serving on the Topeka area Young Life Board of Directors and leading a small group in his church are two of his great joys. The Association of Fundraising Professionals, Topeka Chapter, has recognized Jeff with the Outstanding Volunteer Philanthropist Award for his work in the Topeka Community.

Jeff is married to his high school sweetheart, Sheryl, and together they have three sons: Adrian, a rancher and horse trainer in the Flint Hills of Kansas and his wife, Abbey, have four children; Andrew, the Topeka area director for Young Life and his wife, Angelyn, have three children; and Jon, a financial advisor at CFG,

Inc. and his wife, Brittney, have two children. Jeff and Sheryl love spending time with their active family and friends. They love to garden and travel together.

Jeff thoroughly enjoys his career and actually does not see himself retiring from it. His clients become his friends and he loves helping them pursue their retirement dreams. However, in his own career, he has the freedom to plan his calendar as he desires. Thus, he is blessed to continue in the work he has spent a lifetime pursuing and has the freedom to enjoy.

J on Vogel, an Investment Advisor Representative of CFG Trusted Advisors, Inc. and insurance professional of CFG, Inc., joined his dad at CFG the beginning of 2013. He previously interned with CFG as a financial technician in college, where he learned many of the foundational principles of wealth creation and protection. Jon is dedicated to applying his knowledge of economics to personal wealth management and making a lasting impact in the lives of his clients.

Jon has been married to his beautiful wife, Brittney, for 10 years, and they have two wonderful children: Forest, his 4-year-old son; and Marley, his 2-year-old daughter. When not serving clients of CFG, he enjoys spending time outdoors, working with his hands, and reading. Jon and Brittney both enjoy getting away to the mountains to hike and enjoy God's wondrous creation.

ACKNOWLEDGMENTS

There are so many people I want to give thanks to for without them my life would not be what it is today.

Above all I want to thank my Lord and Savior, Jesus Christ, who has given me eternal and abundant life. He gives me wisdom and insight into things I did not see before, integrity and allows me to have some influence in other people's lives.

Thank you to Sheryl, my wife of 41 wonderful years as of the writing of this book, whose thoughtful insights and gentle nudges have made an unbelievable impact on my life.

To my parents, Harold and Luella Vogel, and Sheryl's parents, Robert and Edna Morlan. These were my first clients 31 years ago. I dearly miss them and appreciate their confidence in me and the wisdom they shared.

Vaughn Kimball, thank you for taking a young man like me and mentoring me in this profession. You were a great example of what it means to care for and advise clients.

Thank you to my three sons: Adrian, for your diligence and pursuit of excellence; Andrew, a man after God's own heart; Jonathan, for the kindness, gentleness and love you show others and for joining me in this great profession. You all three possess all these qualities and are a great example to me, making me a better person.

Thank you to the wives of my sons: Abbey, Angelyn and Brittney, who are like daughters to me, giving me great joy, insight into things that matter, and 10 grandchildren. Thank you for putting up with my new ideas at times.

Thank you to my grandchildren: Paxton, Piper, Lincoln, Lola, Elliot, Tobi (I will see you in heaven), Adelyn, Forest, Marley and Remi. You are my crown and source of many stories. Thank you for allowing me to share them. I pray for you daily (and your future unknown spouses!). As Psalm 127 says, "Behold, children are a heritage from the Lord, the fruit of the womb is a reward. Like arrows in the hand of a warrior, so are the children of one's youth. Happy is the man whose quiver is full of them."

For Robert Castiglione, who saved my career 20 years ago and taught me the truth about how money works in our personal economies. He took on a whole industry and won.

Thank you to my team at CFG, who are always helpful and willing to serve our clients alongside me. Regina Stephenson, who stayed with me and helped me write and edit this book.

Last but not least, thank you to my clients, who have entrusted me with their lives' savings, and without whom none of this would be possible.

CONTACT

Thank you for reading. If you have questions about any of the topics we've covered or if you are searching for a professional who can take a bird's eye view of your finances, we'd be happy to help. You can contact us at:

Jeff Vogel & Jon Vogel
CFG Trusted Advisors, Inc.
www.cfgks.com
785.228.1234 | cfg@cfgks.com

Address:
2820 Mission Woods Dr.
Suite 100
Topeka, KS 66614